P.9. Simple Cone Tree
P.47. Triangle Xmas Tree
P.37 Triangle Star Mobiles.
P.54 Snowman
P.107 Father Xmas.

BRIGHT IDEAS FOR CHRISTMAS ART AND CRAFT

from *Scholastic Magazines*

Ward Lock Educational/Scholastic

CONTENTS

Published by Scholastic Publications (Magazines) Ltd and Ward Lock Educational Co Ltd.

© 1984 Scholastic Publications (Magazines) Ltd

Ward Lock Educational Co Ltd
47 Marylebone Lane, London W1A 6AX
A Ling Kee Company

Scholastic Publications (Magazines) Ltd
9 Parade, Leamington Spa
Warwickshire CV32 4DG

Ideas drawn from Scholastic's magazines, including *Child Education*, *Junior Education* and *Art and Craft*.

Compiled by Audrey Vincente Dean
Edited by Anne Faundez
Illustrations by Jill Clark

ISBN 0-7062-4454-0

Front cover: Crystal forms, Oxford Scientific Films.
Back cover: Crystal forms, Oxford Scientific Films.

INTRODUCTION

The ideas suggested in this book are meant to be used as launching platforms. They can be elaborated upon or simplified, made smaller or larger. In many cases, precise measurements have not been given because often the design may be tailored according to the resources available. For instance, the snowman Advent calendar on page 53 can be given a muffler made from striped material, a woolly one, or a paper version with the school colours on it. The packing-case crib on page 82 can be made from any box to suit figures of all sizes. Other suggestions are given in the follow-up sections.

The age ranges given are only meant as a general guide. The word *upwards* after an age range indicates that the idea is capable of further development, particularly in the case of Christmas-tree ornaments, which offer much scope for decoration. The words *with help* are self-explanatory: sometimes the teacher and more able children will be able to do some of the work, while the others contribute.

The book is not only meant to be used in schools, it is also for parents, who will find it invaluable as a source of ideas. I made the decorate-the-tree calendar for my own three children, in which there is five years' difference between the eldest and the youngest. For several years they took turns in having the privilege of placing the day's ornament on the appliqué tree, and the calendar was a treasured feature of the Christmas season. Parents may find here many creative ideas which will help to keep the children happily occupied; a sure way of ensuring their own peace of mind.

Audrey Vincente Dean

5

CHRISTMAS TREES FOR TABLE DECORATIONS

Small trees

Natural branch tree

Age range
Five to seven.

Group size
Individuals.

What you need
A bare branch or twigs; Plasticine; one yoghurt pot; a piece of cork bark; white emulsion paint or detergent powder; glitter powder; small decorations or beads.

What to do
A bare branch often has a delightful twiggy quality that suggests a small tree. Tiny nativity figures would look well placed under it to form a little scene. For the very smallest trees, use a spray of grape stalks. First, plant the tree in its pot, or weight it with Plasticine. Pieces of cork bark, obtainable cheaply from garden centres, can be used as natural rock-like bases. To recreate snow-laden branches, dab white emulsion paint here and there and sprinkle them with glitter powder while they are still wet. (See 'Techniques' for ideas on handling this powder). Detergent powder, mixed with water to a thick creamy consistency, is an alternative to emulsion paint. The tree should not be touched, for after the powder has dried it will fall off. The tree may be decorated with beads tied on to loops of thread or with other ornaments to scale. Lumps of moss held in place with tooth picks, pine-cone scales and tiny red toadstools, which can be bought, may be fixed on to the tree base.

Pine-cone tree

Age range
Five to seven.

Group size
Individuals.

What you need
One large pine-cone; white emulsion paint; one discarded paper or plastic drinking cup; plaster filler or plaster of Paris and a mixing bowl; felt-tipped pens; coloured paper; a star for the tree-top; glitter powder; contact adhesive; sequins or tinsel braids.

What to do
Trim the cup to a little less than half the height of the pine-cone. Decorate it, for example with a zigzag design drawn with felt-tipped pens, or made from bands of coloured paper, sequins or tinsel braids.
   Mix some plaster filler with water till it is the consistency

7

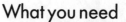

of thick double cream and fill the cup to within 3 cm of the rim, then plant the base of the cone in it. Do not fill up the cup completely otherwise the filler will ooze over the top. Leave it to set; this will take a few days. Much quicker results can be obtained with plaster of Paris, but this is more difficult to handle. Measure the water from the cup and pour it into the mixing bowl (preferably one that can be discarded). Add the powder to the water, sifting it in until a peak of powder can be seen breaking the surface of the water. Mix gently, then pour the mixture immediately into the cup, as it sets very quickly. Allow the surplus to set in the mixing bowl, then throw it away. If the bowl is not disposable, flex the sides to free the plaster – do not pour it in a liquid state down the sink or you will block the drains. Paint the opened pine-cone scales white, as for the natural

branch tree described above, and stick a fancy star to the top of the tree with contact adhesive. For ideas on making the star, see the relevant section in the chapter 'Stars for the tree-top'.

8

Drinking-cup tree

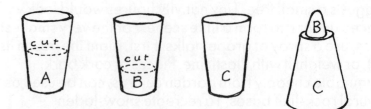

Age range
Five to seven.
Seven to nine.

Group size
Individuals.

What you need
Three discarded drinking cups – those made of expanded polystyrene are the easiest to manage; tissue-paper in two colours, one for the pot and the other for the tree; adhesive; glitter powder, sequins or self-adhesive stars.

What to do
Select two contrasting colours of tissue-paper. Red and green are the traditional colours, but a fantasy tree, say pale pink or white, would be fun, with a bright pink or pale-coloured cup for the pot. Trim two cups, one to measure approximately 6.5 cm in height (A) and the other to measure approximately 3 cm (B). These are for the tub and the tree-top respectively. Take cup B and snip from the lower edge to the centre of the top and press it into a cone shape, then stick it to the top of the untrimmed cup (C), as shown, to make the structure for the tree.

Cover the tub cup (A) with a square or circle of tissue, tuck the surplus inside it, then decorate the outside. Fold a sheet of tissue into four and cut strips about 3 cm wide, or trim strips from an unfolded packet of tissue. Make close snips into one long edge of the folded strips and open them out so that the paper remains double. With practice you will be able to cut long strips of folded paper quite quickly. Starting at the bottom, spread glue over the cup and wind the strips round in a spiral, so that the tree structure is completely covered.

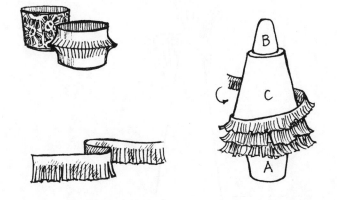

Decorate the outside of the tree with adhesive and glitter powder, or stick on large sequins or self-adhesive stars. Spread glue on the inside of the tree at the bottom and press it on to the tub, which may be weighted inside with a lump of Plasticine.

Small cone trees

The cone is such a useful shape to suggest a Christmas tree that many versions can be invented. Here are some.

Simple cone tree

Age range
All ages.

Group size
Individuals.

What you need
Thin coloured card; felt-tipped pens; paints; glitter powder; foil; gummed-paper shapes and a doily to decorate; adhesive; a short tube; a ruler; a pair of compasses.

What to do
This simple cone tree can be made by the youngest child. It can be made to any size and offers great scope for decoration. Crayoning or painting is best done before the cone is raised. Draw a circle on to the card with compasses. Cut it out then cut it into four. When it is folded

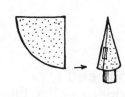

and the edges are stuck down with a slight overlap, each quadrant becomes a tall thin tree. Use half a circle to

9

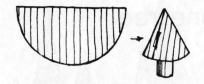

make a tree with a wide base. Make the trunk from a short tube. Do this by curving another piece of card (see 'Techniques') before rolling it. Stick the cone on to the trunk with plenty of glue.

Ways in which the cone can be decorated are shown in the illustration. Use gummed-paper shapes, stick on crumpled foil or spray or stencil it through a paper doily. You may also decorate it with crumpled tissue, milk-bottle tops or gift-ribbon roses.

Fringed-paper cone tree

Age range
Seven to nine upwards.

Group size
Individuals.

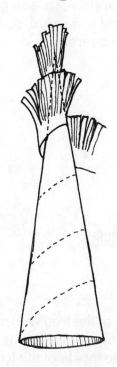

What you need
Tissue-paper, or other thin pliable paper, in different shades of colour; thin card to make the cone; scraps of coloured card; adhesive or Sellotape.

What to do
This tree can be any size but, because of the way the layers of fringed paper hang, it would be best to make it between 30 and 45 cm tall. Cut out a half-circle from thin card, with the radius equalling the desired height of the tree, and curve it with a ruler – see 'Techniques' page 87. Curve it

round firmly so that the card is double and shape it into a tall thin cone. Apply glue or Sellotape to hold the form in place. Make the width of the fringed-paper strips approximately one-fifth of the height of the cone. Place four or five sheets of tissue, or thin pliable paper, on top of one another and cut them to the width required. Then fold them and fringe the edges as described for the drinking-cup tree on page 9, snipping to within 3 cm of the opposite edge. Do not separate the layers. Spread glue over the tip of the cone and hold it in the left hand so that the tip points downwards. Apply the layers of fringed paper with the right hand, with the uncut edge pointing towards the base of the cone. Begin sticking at the tip of the cone to ensure that this part is covered and work round the tree towards its base in a spiral fashion.

The drawing of the finished tree will give you an idea of the spacing of the layers. When the tree is upright the layers will flop downwards in a decorative shape.

Pyramid tree

Age range
Seven to nine.

Group size
Individuals.

What you need
Two 14.5-cm squares of paper, coloured on one side and white on the other; foil; one cotton-reel; pencil; a length of dowel or a paper spill.

What to do
This pretty tree is already decorated since it relies for its effect on the choice of colours used in its layers. Draw the pattern from the diagram and fold along the dotted lines.

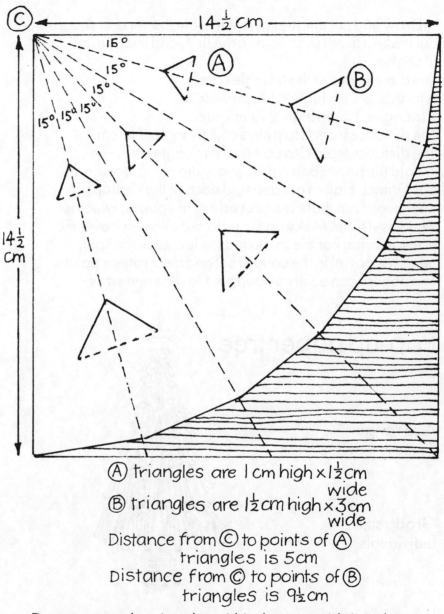

Ⓐ triangles are 1 cm high × 1½ cm wide

Ⓑ triangles are 1½ cm high × 3 cm wide

Distance from Ⓒ to points of Ⓐ triangles is 5 cm

Distance from Ⓒ to points of Ⓑ triangles is 9½ cm

Do not cut out the triangles within the pyramid. Join the edges on the underside with a strip of Sellotape. This is the inner pyramid.

* A template is provided on page 123

Draw and cut another pyramid from the second square, but make it 5 mm shorter than the first, and include the triangles.
The dimensions of the triangles are:
A triangles 1 cm high × 1.5 cm wide.
B triangles 1.5 cm high × 3 cm wide.
The distance from C to points of A triangles is 5 cm.
The distance from C to points of B triangles is 9.5 cm.

Fold the paper and cut the triangular slits, leaving the base intact. Flatten out and fold each of the six flaps downwards so that the underside of the paper, which is white, is visible. Make up the pyramid and slip it over the previous one. For the trunk and the tub, stick the spill, pencil or dowel in the cotton reel and decorate or paint it. The pattern can easily be adapted to different sizes.

Pop-up paper tree

Age range
Seven to nine.

Group size
Individuals.

What you need
One unopened roll of green crêpe paper; adhesive; glitter powder; discarded paper cup or yoghurt pot for the tub.

What to do
This tree is very quick to make. It is a version of an old party trick. The finished tree looks more like a palm tree until it is snipped into shape. You need to experiment before arriving at exactly the size you want, so you might like to practise on newspaper first. Double crêpe paper, with a different shade of green on each side, makes an attractive tree. Cut the unopened roll to a width of about 18 cm and, without undoing it, cut close fringes into it about 8 cm deep, then unfold the paper. Lay the piece on a flat surface, one short end towards you and roll it up, not too tightly, round a pencil, keeping the uncut edges level.

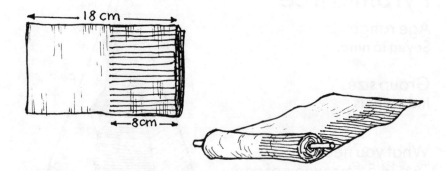

Remove the pencil and take hold of the fringed centre with your right forefinger and thumb, while holding the other end in your left hand. Gently pull the centre upwards and at the same time twist it in an anticlockwise direction. You will find that the tree begins to grow. Ease out the layers bit by bit, then add a dab of glue to the bottom layer to hold it in place, or twist it securely. Trim it into shape. Decorate the tree with glitter, plant it in its tub, and wedge the base in place with bits of crumpled tissue.

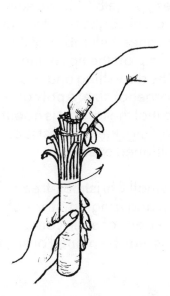

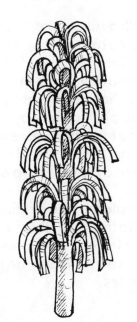

netting into a cone and tie it to the tub with the string. Take the paper doilies and crunch them up a little in the middle, then insert the points, pushing them through the mesh of the wire netting until it is completely covered. You may also use circles of tissue-paper or foil cut to different sizes. Alternatively, use transparent plastic bags cut into fringes instead of paper or foil.

Larger cone trees

Wire-netting cone tree

Age range
Seven to nine upwards.

Group size
Small group.

What you need
A waste-paper basket for the tub; a length of wire netting with large mesh; a length of string; paper doilies; tissue-paper; foil or crêpe paper.

What to do
Make the tub by covering the outside of the waste-paper basket with baking foil or crêpe paper. Form the wire

13

Tiered cone tree

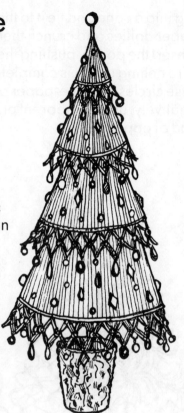

Age range
Nine to twelve.

Group size
Small group.

What you need
Thin dowelling, 50 cm long; an empty can for the tub; thin coloured card; adhesive; dark brown or black paint; foil or tissue-paper to decorate; textured paper, felt or other material that does not fray; beads; fringing, gold cord or other shiny trimmings.

What to do
Paint half the dowelling dark brown or black. Decorate the outside of the can and fill it with Plasticine. You may also use plaster filler or plaster of Paris instead of Plasticine – see the instructions for the pine-cone tree, page 7. Plant the dowelling firmly with the painted part at the bottom. Draw four half-circles on the coloured card, with a radius of 22 cm, 16 cm, 14 cm and 12 cm respectively. Cut out these half-circles. Use them as patterns to cut out the same shapes in textured paper, felt, jersey or towelling (this step may be omitted). Curve each

card with a ruler – see 'Techniques', page 87. Shape each into a cone by overlapping the straight edges slightly and sticking them together. Cover the cones with fabric at this point if you have chosen to use it. Snip off the tips of the cones so that they fit tightly on to the dowelling and slide them into position one by one, in order of size. Apply glue inside the ends and place them so that the largest is about 30 cm from the bottom of the dowelling, the smallest is at the top, and the other two are positioned evenly in between.

Decorate the tree by sticking a small Christmas-tree bauble to the top of the dowelling; add fringing, strips of paper or felt cut into points, to the edges of each cone. Glass jewels, foil, and large beads may be pinned or stuck to the cones.

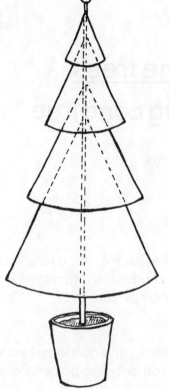

Alternatively, instead of covering the cones with fabric, cut four circles of stiff foil, one for each cone. Make the radius a little larger than for the cones. Place the circle on a padded surface, wrong side upwards and using a blunt point such as an empty ballpoint pen, score on it the lines and pattern illustrated.* Fold the circle in four, and snip off the point. Unfold the circle, flatten it out and cut out the pattern, cutting from the outside to the centre. Slip it over the appropriate cone, arranging it so that the points are raised. For the smaller circles, you may find it easier to use a four-point design rather than the six-point one shown.

* A template is provided on page 126

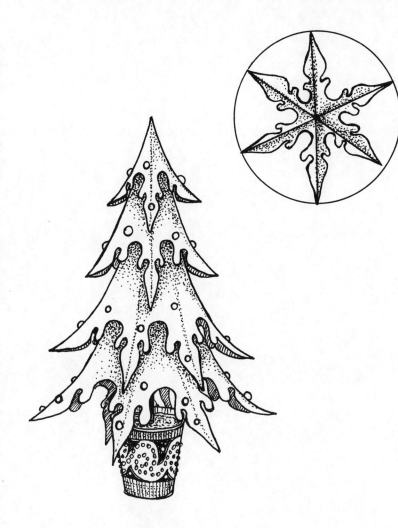

Eggshell cone tree

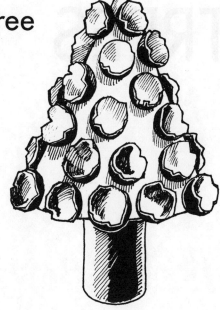

Age range
Nine to twelve.

Group size
Small group.

What you need
Thin card, preferably coloured; a tube, section of a tube, large can or waste-paper basket; eggshells cut in half; metallic spray paint.

What to do
Make a large cone from half a circle. (See 'Techniques', page 92, for how to draw a large circle without compasses.) Use coloured card if possible so that any spaces left after the subsequent spraying will look decorative rather than bare or patchy. For the base, cover a large can or waste-paper basket, or make a tube, bearing in mind the proportion of the cone. A weight inside gives it stability. Glue the eggshells to the cone and spray the whole with metallic paint.

LARGE CHRISTMAS TREES

Two-dimensional newspaper tree

Age range
Nine to twelve.

Group size
Groups or individuals.

What you need
Old newspapers;
cold-water paste;
a large can or pot
for the tub; paint or
metallic spray to
decorate.

What to do
Sometimes there is no space
for a three-dimensional
Christmas tree, although the
children would like to make
the traditional decorations. Here is an idea for a flat tree
which remains free-standing. Roll each double sheet of
newspaper into a spill, following the instructions for the
three-dimensional newspaper tree, but do not fringe the
edges. Tear narrow strips of newspaper and paste them,
then take three or four spills and wind the pasted strips
round them to make the central trunk. Arrange the
branches so that they consist of single spills, evenly
spaced, or groups of spills.

Fix each spill or group of spills in place by bandaging a
strip of paper criss-cross round the trunk, starting at the
bottom. Make the top by placing two or three spills
together and sticking a few more either side of the
remainder of the trunk. Trim the branches into shape.
When it is dry, the tree may be painted or sprayed gold
or silver.

17

Three-dimensional newspaper tree

Age range
Nine to twelve.

Group size
Small or large groups.

What you need
Approximately 30 double
sheets of old newspaper;
a pencil or knitting needle;
Sellotape; crêpe paper;
one waste-paper basket;
scrap paper; card; paint;
a large house-painting brush.

What to do
At little cost you can make a realistic tree, large enough to
take all the traditional trimmings. To make one branch,
open out a double sheet of newspaper and roll it up tightly
to form a firm spill. It is easier if you begin the spill by
rolling the newspaper round a pencil or a thick knitting
needle. Leave the knob of the knitting needle or one end of
the pencil protruding. When only two edges of the
newspaper are visible, snip irregularly into them.

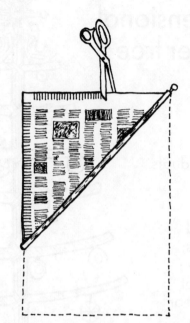

Continue rolling and dab a little glue into the remaining
corner so that the spill will stay in shape. The fringe of the
paper will stick out irregularly to give the effect of pine
needles. Repeat with the other sheets until you have about
30 branches. Make the trunk by taking three spills and
wedging one into the end of another. Bandage round the
joins tightly with Sellotape. This is the centre shoot, A;
repeat twice more to make shoots B and C. Bind them
together with Sellotape round the top and about half-way
down, as illustrated. Make three more spills, not quite as
long, to give added strength lower down. Fasten the
bundle of six spills together with Sellotape, beginning the
binding about 25 cm from the bottom. The free lower ends
represent roots.

Add more tiers of branches made from single spills,
fitting each into the grooves round the trunk and fastening

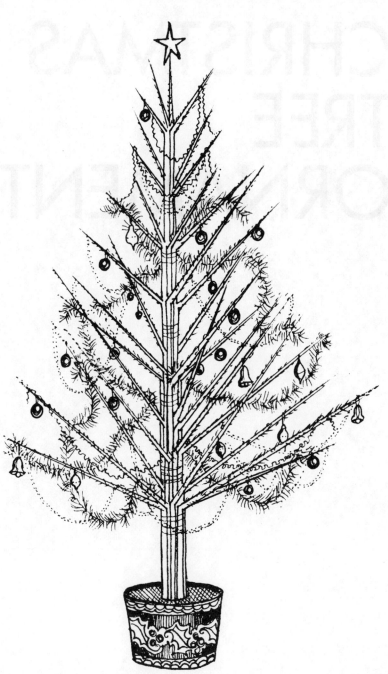

them in place with Sellotape. Bend the roots outwards, as shown, and wedge the tree into a decorated waste-paper basket, which should then be packed firmly with scrap paper and card and, if necessary, weighted so that the tree remains firm. Bend the branches outwards, clipping some of them if required to give the correct shape. When it is complete the tree can be painted.

CHRISTMAS
TREE
ORNAMENTS

Mainly egg cartons

A chime of bells

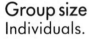

Age range
Five to seven upwards.

Group size
Individuals.

What you need
Egg cartons; silver or gold spray paint; coloured thread; baking foil or Christmas baubles for clappers; yoghurt pots or drinking cups; milk-bottle tops; narrow ribbon or decorative yarn.

What to do
Cut out sections from plastic egg cartons. Spray them silver or gold. To do this lay them near each other and spray them all at once. Pierce a hole in the middle of each section and thread them with decorative yarn or narrow ribbon. Tie on a clapper made from a small Christmas-tree bauble, or mould a piece of baking foil round a large knot or small bead. A cluster of three or four bells hung together on different lengths of yarn looks effective. Knot them together and tie with a bow of ribbon. Use yoghurt pots or drinking cups to make bigger bells. They can be covered with baking foil instead of being sprayed with paint. Make tiny bells from milk-bottle tops moulded round a thimble.

Flowers

Age range
Seven to nine upwards.

Group size
Individuals.

What you need
Egg cartons; foil; pieces of doily; pipe-cleaners; silver or gold paint.

What to do
Use a pastel-coloured plastic egg carton, or a transparent plastic one and spray it with silver or gold paint. Cut out a section and snip it to look like the petals of a flower.

Cut two circles of foil, one about 7.5 cm in diameter and the other 10 cm. Fold each into eight and cut the top of the folded sections into a curve. Unfold them so you have a circle of petal shapes.

Make a hole in the centre of each circle. For the flower centre, bend over 12 mm of one end of a pipe-cleaner and put a drop of glue on it. Make a foil tassel by snipping into one long edge of a piece of foil measuring 2.5 × 15 cm and rolling it round the glued double end of the pipe-cleaner. Thread the egg-carton petals on to the pipe-cleaner behind the tassel, followed by two foil petals. Bend the pipe-cleaner downwards to form a stem.

Alternatively, the centres can be made of small Christmas-tree baubles, or a few centimetres of crumpled-up Christmas-tree garland. You can also enclose a piece of cotton wool in the bent end of the cleaner and gather a circle of crêpe paper round it. Tie a thread underneath to hold the gathering in place.

Egg-box baubles

Age range
Five to seven upwards.

Group size
Individuals.

What you need
An egg carton; spray or poster paint; sequins, glitter powder or braid; adhesive; a length of ribbon or yarn.

What to do
Cut out two sections from an egg carton, make a hole in the centre of one and insert a thread from which to hang

22

the finished bauble. Stick the sections together, paint or spray them, and decorate the outside with glitter, sequins or braid.

Make a bauble with a hanging tassel by inserting a thread through the lower egg cup before gluing the two together. Then make the tassel as for the flower centre described in 'Flowers' and attach it to the thread. Make bigger baubles by gluing two foil cake-cups or two drinking cups together. You can also make a string of baubles by threading them together, one below the other.

Egg-box lantern

Since this ornament may be too large to decorate some trees, it can be made to hang elsewhere; from the ceiling, for example.

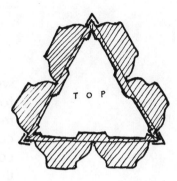

Age range
Five to eleven.

Group size
Individuals.

What you need
Three transparent egg boxes; scraps of coloured tissue-paper; thick thread; adhesive; wide Sellotape; a blunt pointed instrument, such as a knitting needle.

What to do
Put a dab of adhesive in the egg-box sections and fill each with a different colour of crumpled tissue. Pierce a hole in the centre of each of the short sides of the egg boxes.

Smear the long sides with adhesive and glue the three egg boxes together in a triangular shape, reinforcing the joints with Sellotape.

Make a large tassel from several layers of tissue-paper about 20 cm wide. Snip into the long edge and roll the strips into a cylinder, then wind thread round the top to secure it. Push loops of thread through the holes at the top and bottom of the lantern. Tie the tassel to one group of loops, and knot the others together to form a hanger.

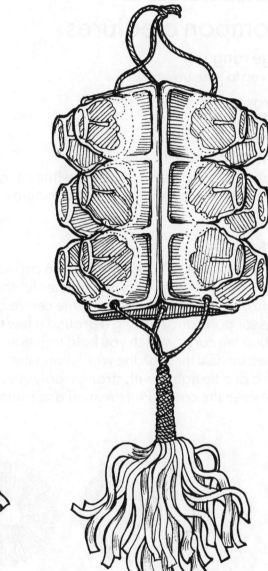

23

Mainly wool

Pompon creatures

Age range
Seven to nine upwards.

Group size
Individuals.

What you need
Thin card; wool; scraps of felt; white fringing and cotton wool for the Father Christmas pompon.

What to do
Cut two circles of card, one about 6 cm in diameter for the body and the other 4 cm in diameter for the head. Make a hole about 2 cm in diameter in the centre by inserting a scissor point and twisting it around a few times. Wind wool round the cards, which you hold together, until the hole is filled up. Cut through the wool along the edge of each card and tie tightly with strong wool round the centre between the cards. Pull them off and trim the resulting ball.

Alternatively, a much quicker, but slightly more difficult, way of making a pompon is to cut out the figure illustrated four times. Since this method results in a ball which needs more trimming to shape than the first, the cards should be cut a little larger in diameter. To start, lay one piece of contrasting wool between each pair of cards and see that the ends remain hanging. Wind the wool round the cards, stopping within the jutting ends of the cards. Tie the ends of the contrast yarn firmly together before cutting the strands. Each semicircle will give half a pompon, and the contrasting lengths should be tied firmly together.

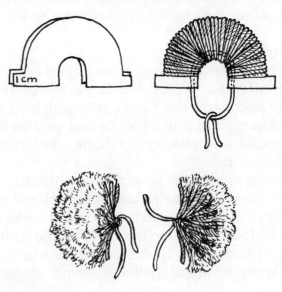

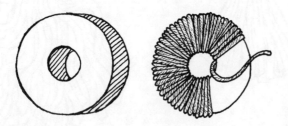

Snowman: make body and head pompons and tie them together with the gathering threads. Make a little hat from a tube and a circle of black felt and decorate it with a sprig of holly made from green felt. Add the facial features, and buttons to the body.

Robin: make a body-sized pompon. Use brown wool around three-quarters of the circle and red wool for the rest. Cut a diamond-shaped piece of brown felt, fold it in half and glue it in place for the beak, add felt eyes, tail and feet.

Father Christmas: make a pompon in pink wool for the head and one in red wool for the body. Tie them together. Add a hat made from a tube of felt gathered at one end with a cotton-wool tassel, and a beard from white fringing or cotton wool. Stick on a belt, features and feet cut from cotton wool.

25

God's eyes

Age range
Nine to twelve upwards.

Group size
Individuals.

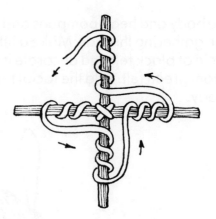

What you need
Wools of different colours and textures; cocktail sticks; thin pieces of dowel or lolly sticks; tinsel yarn, raffia or other fancy thread; foil or paint to cover the stick ends.

What to do
Glue two dowels or lolly sticks together at right angles. Begin wrapping the wool in the centre two or three times in one direction, then crosswise in the other. Continue wrapping each arm consecutively. Wrap twice round each arm from front to back.

End the rounds of one colour on the same arm as you started, and glue the wool to the back of this arm after the last wrap. Then tie another colour to the same place and continue, varying the colours and the textures of the threads as much as possible. Finish when only about 12 mm of each arm is visible. Paint the remainder or glue a scrap of foil over the ends.

Follow-up
Lay three sticks over each other to give a hexagonal ornament, or make one stick of a pair shorter than the other for a diamond shape. Fasten wool tassels or glittery beads to the side arms.

Mainly doilies

Doily bag

Age range
Five to seven upwards.

Group size
Individuals.

What you need
One small white doily; crumpled foil, tissue-paper or sweets; a length of ribbon or tinsel yarn; a small safety-pin; glitter powder and adhesive, or self-adhesive stars.

26

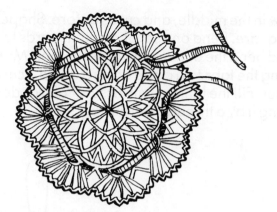

What to do

Fasten a safety-pin to the end of a length of ribbon. Then thread the ribbon in and out near the edge of the doily. Pull the ribbon gently to form a little bag and fill it with crumpled tissue or foil, or insert one or two foil-wrapped sweets. Tie the ends of the ribbon in a loop. Decorate the bag with adhesive stars or dabs of glitter.

Doily bird

Age range
Seven to nine.

Group size
Individuals or small groups.

What you need
Gold or silver doilies; tissue or crêpe paper; thick coloured paper; felt-tipped pens or paints; adhesive; gift ribbon.

What to do
Cut a circle of thick coloured paper, 9 cm in diameter. Make a tassel of tissue or crêpe paper, as for the centres of the egg-box flowers (see page 21). Alternatively, cut and curl a few lengths of gift ribbon – see 'Techniques', page 88. Roll another length of paper to a point for the bird's beak. Spread adhesive on half of one side of the

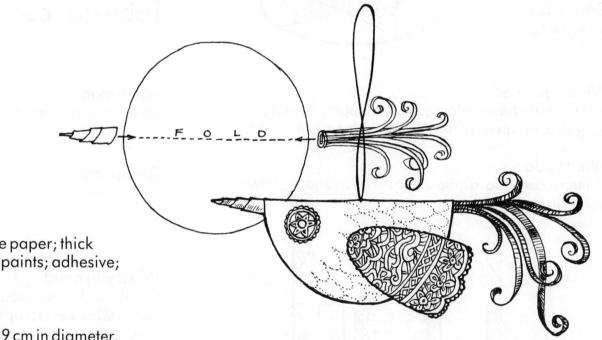

paper and fold it over into a semicircle, enclosing the beak and tail as shown. Cut sections of gold or silver doilies for wings and stick them to the body, and add a round doily flower for each eye. Decorate the breast and eye on both sides with felt-tipped pens or paints.

Mainly card tubes

Lanterns

Age range
Seven to nine upwards.

Group size
Individuals.

What you need
A cardboard tube; coloured tissue-paper; thin card; adhesive; paints or glitter powder; a length of thread.

What to do
Flatten a cardboard tube and cut it to the shape shown in the illustration. Flatten it again so that the cut rectangles

cut away shaded areas

are now in the middle, and cut as before. Shape the roll into a square. Bend one set of points inwards to make the top, and bend the others outwards for tabs. Make the base by gluing the tabs to a circle of card about 7 cm in diameter. Fill the lantern with tissue. Paint or decorate it and hang it by a thread from the top.

Tube dancer

Age range
Seven to nine upwards.

Group size
Individuals.

What you need
Cardboard; tissue-paper or three (or more) doilies; coloured paper; scraps of wool; fabric or ribbons; paints or felt-tipped pens; adhesive.

What to do
Roll a piece of cardboard into a tube measuring 8 cm long and 3 cm in diameter. Paint it. Tangle or plait a length of wool and leave it to dry for a crimped effect. Stick this over

one end of the tube for hair. To make the skirt, cut three or more circles of tissue or doily about 12 cm in diameter. Fold them into quarters and snip off the points so that, when unfolded, they fit tightly on to the tube. Stick them in place one by one. Cut circles of white paper for eyes. Stick them to the tube, then paint or mark in the facial features. Add a ribbon or wool sash above the paper skirts.

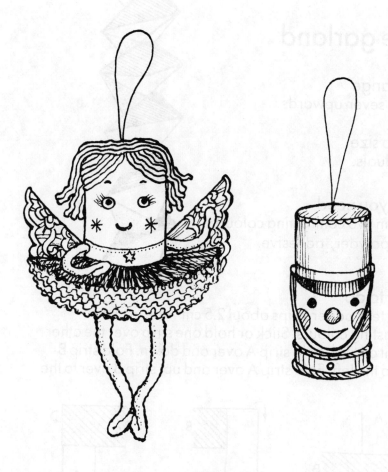

Alternatively, instead of a dancer, make a soldier, clown or fairy for the top of the tree. Add a felt or paper hat to the soldier. These figures may be made more elaborate by covering the tube with paper to suggest a body and by adding pipe-cleaners or strips of felt for arms and legs.

Mainly paper

Tree garland

Age range
Five to seven upwards.

Group size
Individuals.

What you need
Paper in two contrasting colours; glitter powder; adhesive.

What to do
Cut or tear paper strips about 2.5 cm wide in two contrasting colours. Stick or hold one strip over the other at right angles. Fold strip A over and down. Fold strip B over to the left. Fold strip A over and up, strip B over to the

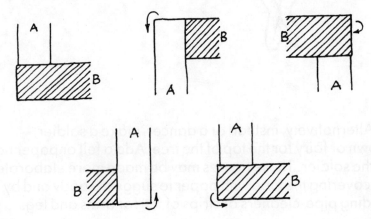

right. Repeat these four movements until you have completed the length of the strips, adding on more as required. You may, if you wish, dip the edges in glue and glitter powder.

Christmas-card star

Age range
Five to seven upwards.

Group size
Individuals.

What you need
Thin card; old Christmas cards; glitter powder; glue; felt-tipped pens.

What to do
Make a template for a star shape by drawing three concentric circles on thin card – say 5 cm, 7 cm and 10 cm in diameter. Join the middle and outer circles with straight lines, as shown. Cut along these lines to make a star shape. Then cut out the centre circle and discard it. The star shape is the front.

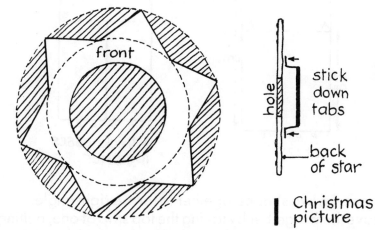

front

hole

stick
down
tabs

back
of star

| Christmas
picture

* A template is provided on page 124

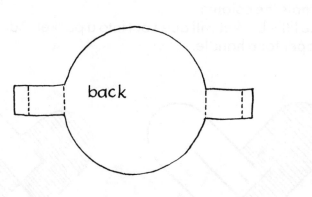

back

For the back, cut a circle 7 cm in diameter with two tabs approximately 4 cm long at each side. Stick a Christmas picture to this circle, bend the tabs and stick them to the wrong side of the front card.

Decorate the front. Make these stars in different sizes to suit the subject-matter of the pictures.

Cake-cup flower

Age range
Five to seven upwards.

Group size
Individuals.

What you need
One *petit four* case; two baking cases for cup-cakes; foil from one chocolate or sweet; gold or silver spray; adhesive.

What to do
Stick the *petit four* case inside one of the cup-cake cases. Turn the other cup-cake case inside out and stick it to the outside of the first. Spray or paint it, then stick the foil, wrapped around a scrap of tissue to make it appear larger, to the centre.

31

Paper-heart basket

Age range
Nine to twelve.

Group size
Individuals.

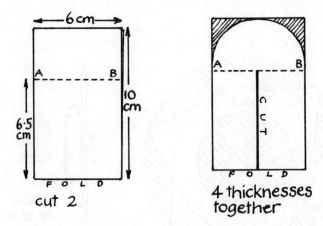

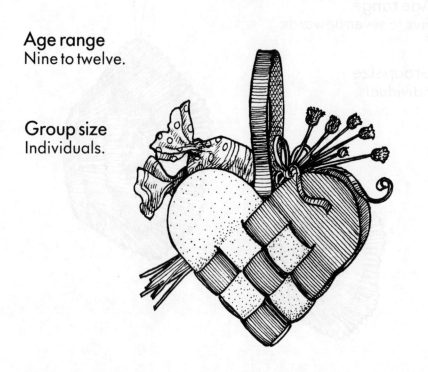

What you need
Paper in two contrasting colours; foil-paper parcels, dried flowers, sweets, etc, to put inside the basket.

What to do
Cut two pieces of paper, each in a contrasting colour and measuring 6 by 20 cm. Fold each in half across the width. Lightly rule in the line A–B on one side only of one piece of paper. Hold both pieces together and cut from the fold to the line A–B. Then cut a semicircle above the line A–B.

cut 2

4 thicknesses together

Place the two shapes together to form a right angle. Weave them together by taking the top strip of one, putting it through the first loop of the other and around the next. Weave the second strip, first around and then through to alternate the colours.

The little basket will open out into a pocket. Add a loop of paper for a handle.

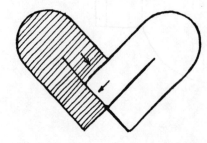

Follow-up
Cut the shapes into three or more strips and weave them together in the same way. You can make the baskets any size as long as the strips are slightly longer than the width of the paper.

Cone Father Christmas

Age range
Seven to nine upwards.

Group size
Individuals.

What you need
A piece of card;
red crêpe or
tissue-paper;
thin white paper;
felt-tipped pens or
paints; adhesive;
cotton wool.

What to do
Draw a circle on to the card. Cut out one third, roll it into the shape of a cone and glue the edges together. Decorate and paint it to suggest a Father Christmas, either the head only or the whole figure. The hat and body may be made from another piece of red tissue or crêpe paper, cut the same shape as the cone and trimmed down, or it may be painted. Decorate the hat with a bobble by adding a tassel of tissue-paper or a tuft of cotton wool. Make a beard from a strip of thin white paper curled and stuck in layers round the bottom of the cone – see 'Techniques', page 88, for the method of curling – or stick on a strip of cotton wool. You may, if you wish, add arms and legs made from flat pieces of paper.

Jelly-case angel

Age range
Seven to nine upwards.

Group size
Individuals.

What you need
One waxed jelly case, with petal-shaped edging; a small polystyrene or paper ball; wool for hair; one sequin; a section of white paper doily; adhesive; felt-tipped pens or paints.

What to do
Cut the jelly case in half, roll it into a cone and glue down the overlapping edges. For the face, make a small hole in the ball to fit the point of the cone, and stick it in place. Add lengths of wool for hair. Add arms made from sections of rolled paper doily. Cut the remainder of the jelly case in two and stick the two halves to the angel's back – these are the wings. Add a little glitter to the body and hair. Mark in the facial features and stick a sequin to the centre of the forehead.

33

Paper fish

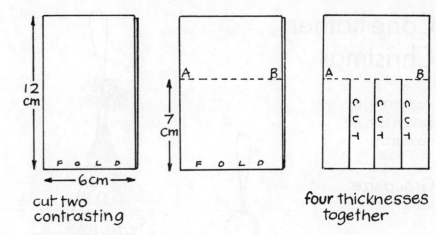

cut two
contrasting

**four thicknesses
together**

Age range
Nine to twelve.

Group size
Individuals.

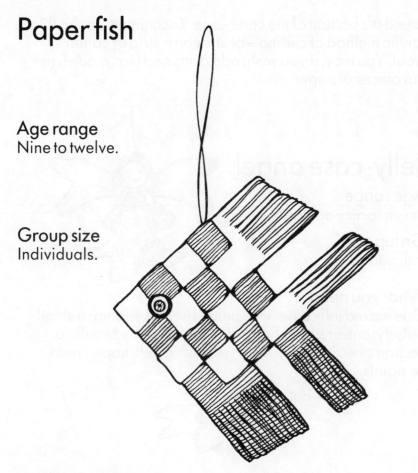

Weave both layers together, as for the paper-heart basket, then cut each end in a slant. Cut away the sections as shown opposite to separate the fins from the tail.

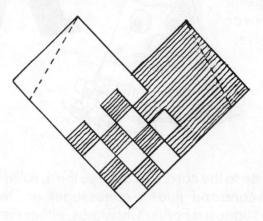

What you need
Paper in two contrasting colours; one sequin or flower cut from a metallic doily, or a felt-tipped pen.

What to do
Cut two pieces of paper, each in a contrasting colour, 6 cm by 24 cm, and fold them in half across the width. On one piece of paper and on one side only, lightly rule the line A–B, 7 cm from the fold. Hold both pieces together exactly and cut out four equal strips.

To make the fins and tail, cut slits in each strip. Make sure the cuts do not go right up to the edge of the woven portion. The fins may now be curled lightly – see 'Techniques', page 88. Mark in the eyes with a felt-tipped pen, or stick a sequin or doily flower in place.

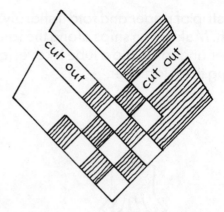

Follow-up
Make these fish any size provided that the length of the strips is greater than the width of the paper. Try making the fins and tail longer. Use foil paper to create a sparkling effect. A strange bird will result if you cut off the lower fin and bend the top two outwards, uncut, to suggest wings.

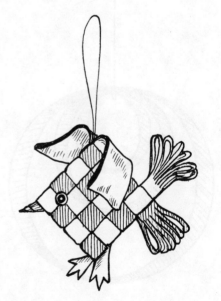

Decorations for a miniature tree

Age range
All ages.

Group size
Individuals.

What you need
Coloured paper; foil; card or stiff paper; sequins; corks; egg boxes; baking foil; gift-wrap ribbon; adhesive; glitter powder to decorate.

What to do
Cork glitter-ball   Tie a thread round a cork by which to hang it, then coat it with adhesive and stick sequins all over it, or roll it in glitter powder.

Spiral Working from the outside inwards, cut into a circle of paper. Hold it by the centre and it will drop into a spiral. Hang it by a thread from the centre.

Lantern Cut a strip of paper and fold it sharply in half along the length. Make even snips along the folded edge. Unfold the paper and roll it into a tube by overlapping the edges and gluing them together.

Ribbon loop Cut three different lengths of self-adhesive gift-wrap ribbon and overlap the ends of each ribbon to form a ring. Stick one inside the other and tie them together with a thread.

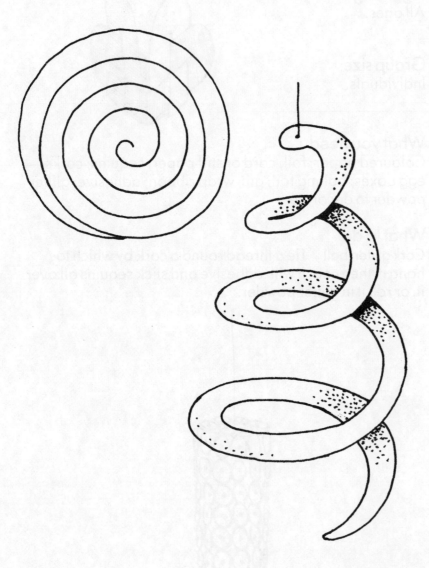

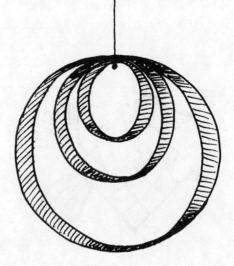

36

Egg-carton basket Cut a section from an egg carton and paint or spray it. Stick a piece of crumpled foil inside. Make a loop of yarn by which to hang the basket.

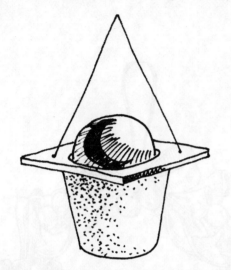

Star Cut two triangles from card or stiff paper and make a shallow slit in the base of each. Press one triangle inside the other and hang them by a thread from the topmost point.

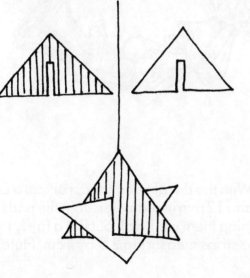

Bakers'-clay decorations

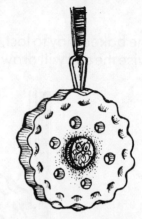

Age range
Five to seven.

Group size
Small group.

What you need
For one batch of clay – four cups of plain flour; one cup of salt; one and a half cups of water; an oven; all kinds of small imprinting tools, such as forks, toothpicks, bottle caps, rounded buttons; paints; varnish; evaporated milk or instant coffee to colour.

What to do
Put the flour, salt and water in a large bowl and mix them together with your hand or a wooden spoon. Although this mixture looks just like pastry it tastes horrible, so attempts to eat it should be discouraged. Knead the 'pastry' on a floured board until it is smooth. Do not try to make upright figures without some kind of framework to hold them up; it is much better to lay them flat on the baking tray. Moisten the joints with water before pressing them together. Make holes for hanging before baking. Place the work in an oven preheated to 170°C (350°F), gas mark 4, and bake it for about one hour, longer if the pieces are thick. Test with a fork or toothpick, inserting it into any joint. If the clay is still soft, leave it in the oven a little longer. To achieve a light-brown leathery look with a slight sheen, paint it with evaporated milk about 30 minutes before baking is complete. If it is kept in the oven longer, the heat will turn it a darker brown, as will painting it more than once. Instant coffee will give a similar colour, but without gloss. If you

37

want the baked clay to last, remember to varnish it, otherwise the salt will draw moisture from the air.

Flat ornaments These can be shaped with biscuit cutters and imprinted by using all kinds of modelling tools. Metal buttons can be pressed into the clay and baked with it.

Holly ring With the flat of your hand, roll out a coil of clay 15 cm long and 12 mm in diameter. Join the ends to make a ring, moistening them well. Roll out flat a fairly thin piece and cut it into strips measuring 2.5 by 4 cm. Flute the strips and moisten the ring. Place the strips on the ring one by one, overlapping them. Add holly berries and a twisted ribbon.

Angel Each piece is made from a separate ball of clay, flattened, shaped and assembled as illustrated. All the joints are moistened before being pressed into place. To dress the angel, roll out a ball of clay about the same size as that used for the body to a thickness of 6 mm. You will create an interesting texture if you roll it out on an old towel. Moisten the body and drape the clay over it. Press into the edges of the wings and dress with the prongs of a fork. Roll and twist small strips of clay for hair. Insert a hook, made from an untwisted and rebent paper-clip, before baking the figure.

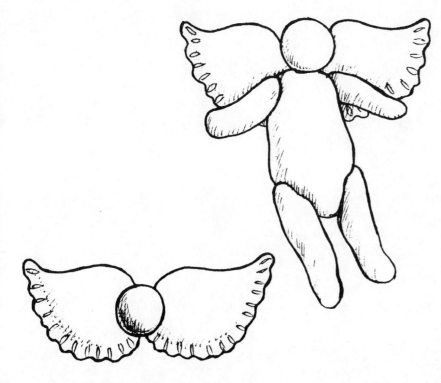

39

STARS
FOR THE
TREE-TOP

Woven-straw star

Age range
Seven to nine
upwards.

Group size
Individuals.

What you need
Drinking straws; tinsel ribbon, raffia or sparkly yarn.

What to do
Divide an even number of drinking straws into four groups and arrange them so that they overlap in the centre.

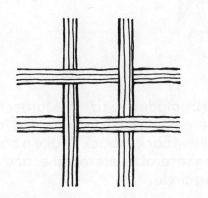

Weave round them with tinsel ribbon, raffia or sparkly yarn for a few turns. Separate all the straws and weave

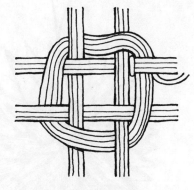

under and over them a few more times. Finish off the weaving and bind the spokes together in pairs. Every other pair may be trimmed short.

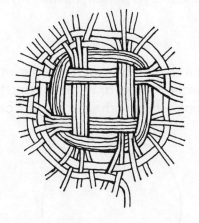

Alternatively, instead of drinking straws, use lengths of cane or coloured pipe-cleaners.

Rayed star

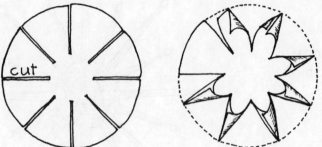

Age range
Nine to twelve.

Group size
Individuals.

What you need
Foil; thin card; adhesive; a pencil (optional); a needle and thread (optional).

What to do
Cut three or four circles of foil, each measuring about 15 cm. Slit each circle at regular intervals and twist the sections into a point, either with your fingers or round a

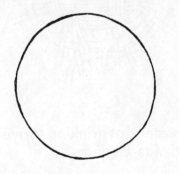

pencil. Stick or sew the circles one on top of the other, bending the points of the top layer upwards. Stick the whole assemblage on to a backing circle of thin card.

Follow-up
These stars can be made any size, the larger they are the more layers are needed. For a hanging star, make two stars and stick them back to back. Make a ball in the same way by stringing several layers together and dispensing with the backing circle.

Cocktail-stick star

Age range
Seven to nine.

Group size
Individuals.

What you need
Card; cocktail sticks;
one paper *petit four* case;
gold or silver spray;
adhesive.

What to do
Cut two thin card circles, each approximately 3 cm in diameter. Spread one card with plenty of adhesive and arrange the ends of 12 to 16 cocktail sticks evenly on it. Apply glue to the other card and sandwich the ends between the two. Stick the *petit four* case to the front card. Spray it with metallic paint and add a foil centre.

Woven-paper star

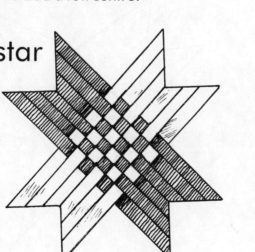

Age range
Five to seven upwards.

Group size
Individuals.

What you need
Paper in two different colours; adhesive.

What to do
Cut four or five paper strips in each colour. Interweave one colour with the other, adding dabs of glue as necessary to keep the weaving in place. Trim the ends as illustrated.

Triangle star

Age range
Seven to nine upwards.

Group size
Individuals.

What you need
Paper; a stapler.

What to do
Cut four equilateral triangles: ABC, CDE, BEF and AFD, to the same size. Hold the four triangles together and fold each angle down to touch the centre of the opposite side. Unfold, and the fold lines will have made a small triangle in the middle.

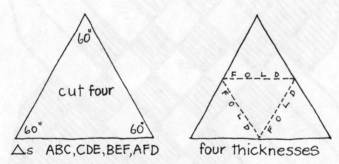

cut four

60° 60° 60°

△s ABC, CDE, BEF, AFD

four thicknesses

FOLD FOLD FOLD

Take ABC as the main triangle. Place AFD directly on top of ABC so that the two angles A are together. Staple along the fold line below angle A. Fit BEF and CDE on to ABC in the same way, stapling along the fold lines below B and C respectively. There will be six loose points remaining. Staple them together along the fold lines, E with E, F with F and D with D.

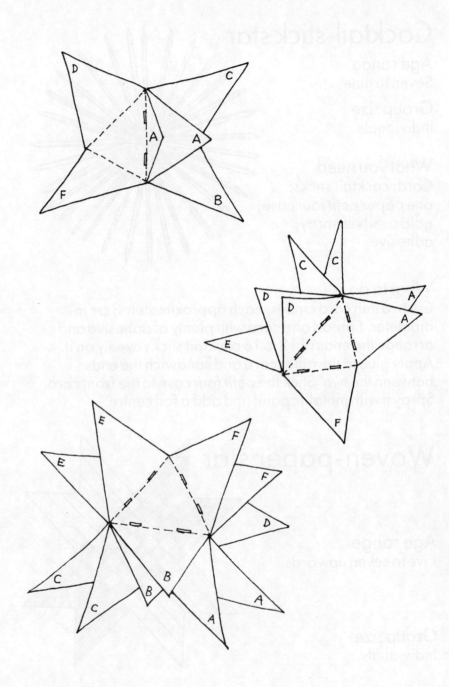

44

ADVENT
CALENDARS

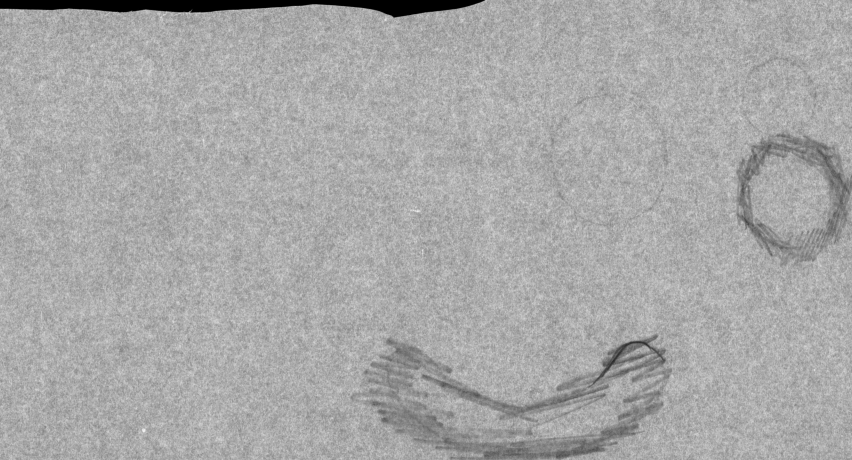

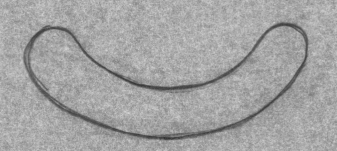

Triangle Christmas-tree calendar

Age range
Five to seven.

Group size
Small group.

What you need
Two 50 × 75 cm sheets of dark-coloured cartridge paper; ten sheets of white A4 typing paper; small pieces of thin paper or foil for snowflakes; one small matchbox or paper doily per child; bits of cord or ribbon; adhesive; a large sheet of thick card and dressmakers' pins, or self-adhesive stars; glitter powder; white paint.

What to do
Glue the two pieces of cartridge paper end to end, overlapping them slightly, to form a large rectangle. Tear or cut each sheet of typing paper in half lengthways and fold each piece in half across the width. Take one of these and, with the fold on the left, rule a line from the top left corner to the bottom right corner and cut along it. You may also cut a jagged edge along the bottom. Open out the paper to give a shallow triangle – this is one bough of your Christmas tree. Cut all but *four* of the other pieces in the same way, then cut four smaller triangles from the remaining paper for the tapering top of the tree. Keeping the fold of each triangle towards you, and beginning at the bottom of the tree, stick or pin each bough to the

background by its two outer tips only, so that it is not stretched out flat. Overlap some of the boughs to suggest an irregular shape and place the four smaller triangles at the top of the tree.

To make each snowflake, fold a small square of thin paper or foil in half twice to give four thicknesses, then fold it diagonally. Cut off the shaped part, then cut irregularly into the folds, as illustrated. Open out the paper and you have a snowflake. Try using tissue-paper, tearing the pieces away to give a soft effect, or cut

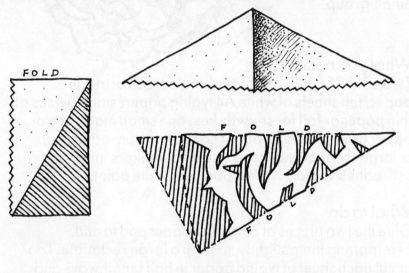

snowflakes from two squares of foil, one a little bigger than the other, and mount the larger one underneath the smaller one. Stick the snowflakes around the tree, and add small crosses or dots of white paint to suggest falling flakes. Put a small present or sweet in each matchbox or in the centre of a paper doily (through the edge of which you can thread a length of cord or ribbon, drawing it up to form a pouch), adding dabs of glue and glitter to decorate. Gift-wrap the matchboxes, tie a loop of tinsel to each and pin them to the tree or stick them on with a

48

self-adhesive star. Attach the doily pouches likewise. Depending on the number of children involved, you may like to number the presents from 1 to 25 or label each with a child's name.

Alternatively, instead of presents, cut out 25 circles of coloured card, number them on one side and stick Christmas scenes on the other side. Suspend the circles from ribbon and fix these to the tree with the numbers facing outwards; turn each over to display the pictures on the appropriate day.

Matchbox Advent calendar

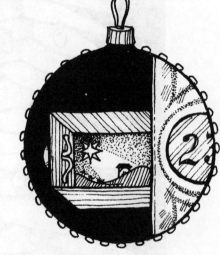

Age range
Five to seven (with help).
Seven to nine.

Group size
Individuals or whole class.

What you need
A piece of stout cardboard, 42 × 15 cm; 25 small matchboxes; 25 prong-type paper-fasteners; 25 adhesive stars or circles large enough to carry numerals; coloured cartridge paper; cut-out pictures or decorations; adhesive; small presents, sweets or pictures from old Christmas cards.

What to do

Stick coloured paper to one side of your piece of cardboard and decorate it. Remove the trays from all the matchboxes and arrange the outer boxes as illustrated,

```
┌──┐   ┌──┐
│ 1│   │ 2│
└──┘   └──┘
┌──┐   ┌──┐
│ 3│   │ 4│
└──┘   └──┘
┌──┐   ┌──┐
│ 5│   │ 6│
└──┘   └──┘
┌──┐   ┌──┐
│ 7│   │ 8│
└──┘   └──┘
┌──┐   ┌──┐
│ 9│   │10│
└──┘   └──┘
┌──┐   ┌──┐
│11│   │12│
└──┘   └──┘
┌──┐   ┌──┐
│13│   │14│
└──┘   └──┘
┌──┐   ┌──┐
│15│   │16│
└──┘   └──┘
┌──┐   ┌──┐
│17│   │18│
└──┘   └──┘
┌──┐   ┌──┐
│19│   │20│
└──┘   └──┘
┌──┐ ┌──┐┌──┐
│21│ │25││22│
└──┘ └──┘└──┘
┌──┐   ┌──┐
│23│   │24│
└──┘   └──┘
```

spacing them evenly to fit under your piece of card. Next, glue the tops of each outer box to the cardboard, lining up the outside edges with the edge of the card. Stick numbered adhesive stars or circles on the front of the card beside each matchbox shell. Glue a small picture inside each matchbox tray, then pierce a small hole at one end of each tray and push a paper-fastener through, splaying the ends out on the inside. Place a sweet or small present in each tray if desired, and insert the trays into the drawers with the paper-fastener handles on the outside. Attach to the top of the calendar some wool or ribbon with which to hang it.

Drum-shaped Advent calendar

Age range
Seven to nine (with help).
Nine to twelve.

Group size
Large group or whole class.

What you need
Two sheets of white card; two sheets of
yellow cartridge paper; 24 Christmas
pictures, each 5 × 5 cm; one special
picture, 5 × 9 cm; felt-tipped pens;
adhesive; scissors.

What to do
To make the under layer, glue the
sheets of white card together end to
end, overlapping them slightly, and cut
to form a rectangle measuring 29 ×
65 cm. Lie this out flat and rule it lightly,
as illustrated. Cut a border out of the
top 3 cm and decorate it.

50

In each of the 5-cm squares have the children either draw or stick a Christmas picture, reserving the special one for the large space. Some suggestions for pictures are: an angel; Santa Claus; stars; the three wise men; the shepherds; a donkey; reindeer; a sleigh; carol singers; parcels; a Christmas tree; Christmas baubles; bells; a Christmas cracker; a paper-chain; a Christmas stocking; a turkey; a plum pudding; party hats; holly; a candle; a snowman; Christmas flowers; a church; and, of course, for Christmas Day itself, a baby in a manger.

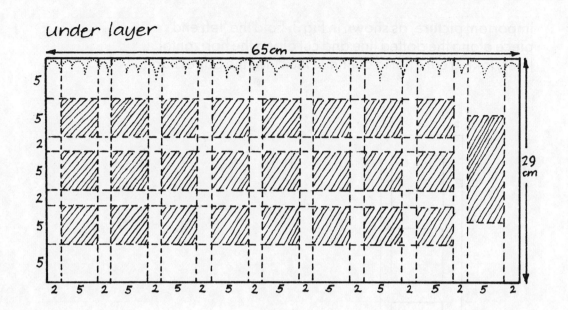

under layer

The upper layer is planned so that the windows can be cut out easily with scissors. Rule the yellow cartridge paper into eight sections measuring 23 × 7 cm and one section measuring 23 × 8 cm and cut them out. Write 'left end' on the back of the bigger piece and rule it as shown in Fig 1. Rule seven of the other pieces as shown in Fig 2 and the remaining piece, which will frame the most

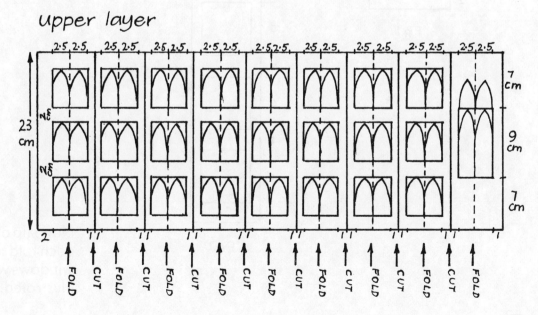

upper layer

51

important picture, as shown in Fig 3. Fold the 'left end' piece along the dotted line and cut along the horizontal lines, taking care not to continue the cut to the paper edge.

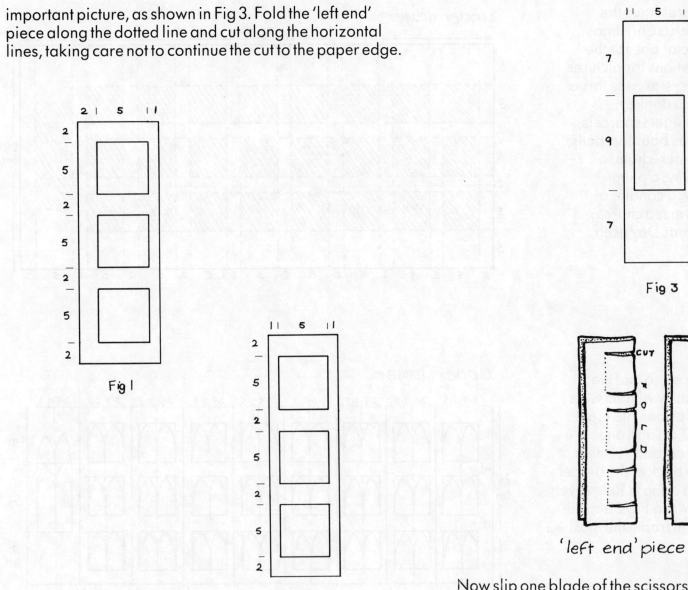

Fig 1

Fig 2

Fig 3

'left end' piece _____

Now slip one blade of the scissors under the wider part of each fold and cut vertically along the fold so that the windows will open outwards like two shutters, as illustrated. Fold each remaining piece vertically and cut them in the same way. Draw a little Gothic window on the outside of each flap using a felt-tipped pen.

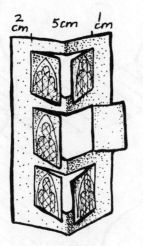

Assemble the calendar by smearing a little glue on the wrong side of the frame of the 'left end' piece, and stick this so that the left edge coincides with the left edge of the under layer, and the flaps open out to reveal the pictures. Continue in the same manner with each of the other frames, placing them edge to edge. Any gaps may be inked in with felt-tipped pen or you may stick a narrow, coloured border over any discrepancies. There will be 1 cm of the under layer remaining uncovered on the right edge. Number the doors from 1 to 25, then curve the calendar into a drum shape and glue the left edge over the uncovered right edge.

Snowman fabric Advent calendar

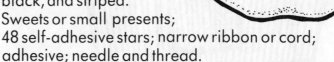

Age range
Nine to twelve.

Group size
Small groups.

What you need
Suggested fabrics: felt, heavyweight Vilene (plain and coloured) or jersey. Colours required: white (at least 60 cm in length), red, black, and striped. Sweets or small presents; 48 self-adhesive stars; narrow ribbon or cord; adhesive; needle and thread.

What to do
To accommodate all the pockets, the snowman needs to be at least 60 cm high, top hat inclusive. Make sure your chosen fabrics have enough body to stay flat and firm — stitch a backing to the snowman and top hat if necessary. Sketch the basic shape of the snowman and cut it out in white fabric. Cut the top hat out of black fabric and use a

53

strip of red fabric (stitched on in four divisions to make pockets) for the hatband. Make a larger pocket out of the

red fabric and sew it to the middle of the top hat. Next, stitch the top hat to the head and add the facial features, making the bowl of the pipe into another pocket.

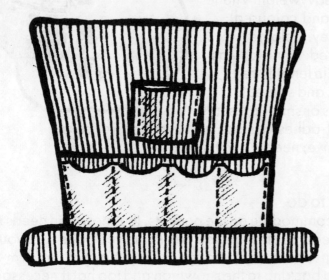

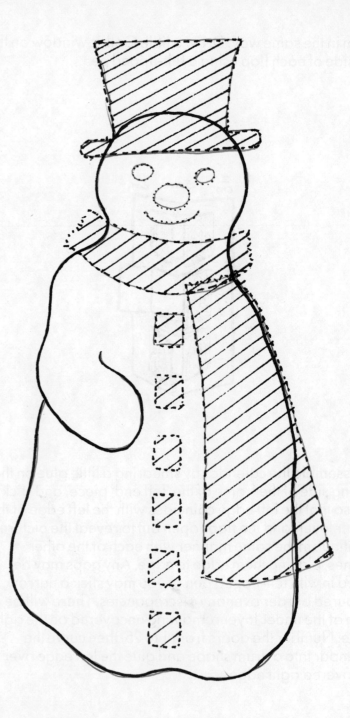

Cut out of striped material the part of the scarf which is to be draped around the snowman's neck and add three pockets to it. Take the ends of this part of the scarf around

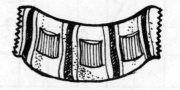

the free edge of the part encircling the neck. Cut another strip for the other free end of the scarf; gather its upper edge slightly and tack it behind the snowman's neck. A fringe attached to the bottom of the scarf adds a finishing touch. Sew on six more pockets, cut from black fabric, down the snowman's front.

to the back of the neck and tack them down, leaving the upper and lower edges of the front free. Cut a longer piece of scarf material for the piece which hangs down the front and sew on another ten pockets in the positions illustrated. Tack it into position, hiding the top edge under

To mark the sweets or presents, cut strips 15–20 cm long of red cord or ribbon. Write the numbers 1 to 25 twice on adhesive gold stars and pair them, sandwiching the ends of the ribbon or cord between them. Tie a small present or sweet to the other end of the ribbons and put them in the pockets, starting with 1 at the bottom and working up to 25 on the top hat. Sew two loops of ribbon or a curtain ring to the top of the snowman so that you can hang up your calendar, or you may prefer to stick the finished figure on a cardboard backing or pin it to the wall.

Decorate-the-tree calendar

Age range
Nine to twelve.

Group size
Small group.

What you need
1.5 m background fabric, 90 cm wide;
70 cm green fabric or felt, 90 cm wide;
a piece of brown fabric, 14 × 15 cm;
a piece of red fabric, 18 × 36 cm;
two dowels; 2 m hat elastic; 24 small
hooks or safety-pins; two curtain
rings; scraps of coloured felt; ribbon;
gold and red ricrac braid; sequins;
a star or fairy for the top of the tree;
red velvet ribbon or strips of red felt
for candles; glass jewels or beads for
flames; gold felt or velvet for candle
haloes; adhesive or sewing equipment.

What to do
Cut 1 m of background fabric, turn a
narrow hem down the sides and make
2.5-cm deep turnings at the top and
bottom for the dowels. Cut the pattern
for the tree from squared paper
following the diagram given. Use this
to cut the tree from the green fabric
and pin it in position on the background,
then stitch or stick it down. If you are

56

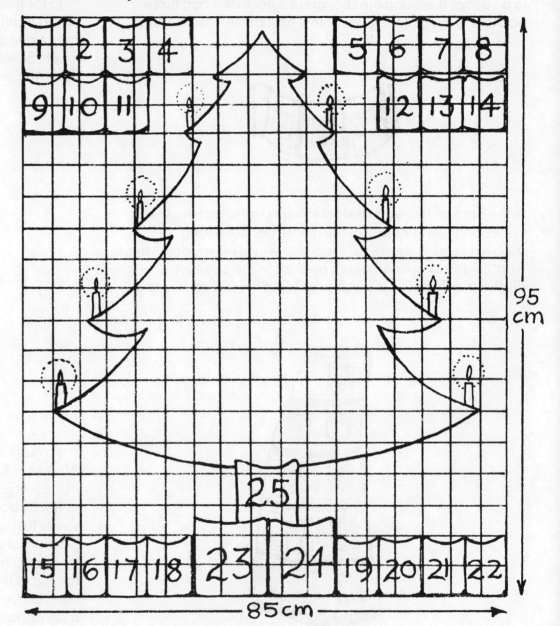

each square = 5cm

95 cm

85 cm

using small hooks to attach your decorations, sew them randomly all over the tree. Cut out circles of gold felt or velvet about 5 cm in diameter and stick or stitch these above the tops of the branches to represent candle haloes. For the candles, cut strips of red felt 6 × 2 cm and stick or sew these on to the tips of the branches, adding a glass jewel or bead to represent the flame. Make tree decorations to hang on the hooks or attach with safety-pins — you may like to make some snowflakes out of brightly-coloured felt, foil or paper, as described on page 48. Attach one or two garlands made from gold and red ricrac braid, and fasten a star or fairy to the top of the tree (or you may like to keep it to put in one of the more important pockets).

To make the pockets, cut four strips of background material each 14 × 48 cm, and two strips each 14 × 36 cm. The other pockets are made from the strip of red fabric, 18 × 36 cm, and the piece of brown fabric 14 × 15 cm. Press under a 12-mm turning on one long side and both short sides of each strip and sew a 2-cm hem on

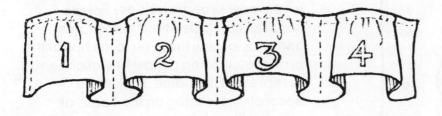

the remaining long side. Cut four 23-cm lengths of hat elastic and thread one through each upper hem of the longer strips. Cut three 15-cm lengths of elastic for each of the shorter pockets, and one 6-cm length for pocket number 25. Sew the ends of the elastic in place. Pleat all the pockets as illustrated and tack them. Cut numerals out of felt and stick these in place on the pockets. Top-stitch the pockets to the background round the lower and shorter edges and up the centre of each inverted pleat. Sew a couple of curtain rings to the top of the calendar with which to suspend it.

Mirror Advent calendar

Age range
Nine to twelve.

Group size
Small group.

What you need
One large sheet of green card; an equally large sheet of paper or plain card covered with baking foil; 25 small Christmas pictures or drawings; felt-tipped pens or paints; sequins; flat shiny decorations; a craft knife; a pair of compasses.

What to do

Cut out a template for the tree shape. (The squared diagram given for the decorate-the-tree calendar on page 56, may be useful.) Draw around it on to the green card and also on to the mirror card. Draw 25 circles on the green card tree; these need not be all the same size. Number the circles and cut round each with a craft knife, leaving a small section of the circle intact on the left side to act as a hinge. On the back of each circle, stick a Christmas picture or drawing – see the drum-shaped calendar on page 50 for picture ideas. Stick the green tree over the mirrored one, placing it slightly lower than the mirrored card so that a shiny edge shows, as illustrated. Take care not to put any adhesive on the back of the doors. Decorate the tree with sequins or flat shiny decorations, such as the foil snowflakes described in the triangle Christmas tree calendar.

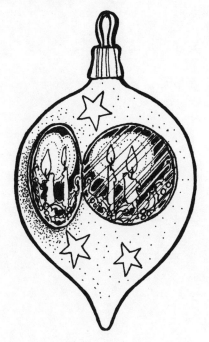

NATIVITY
FIGURES

Folded-card figures

Age range
Five to seven.

Group size
Individuals.

What you need
Strong cartridge paper;
paints or crayons; scissors; foil;
cotton wool; paper doilies.

What to do
Fold in half a square or rectangle of cartridge paper and
cut out a triangle to form the body. The face and arms are
also cut from folded pieces of paper. A nose can be cut
from a folded piece of paper and stuck in place. Add
cloaks, crowns or wings in the same way. Hair and beards
can be made of cotton wool. Two or three paper doilies,
used together for extra strength, give a decorative touch
to angels.

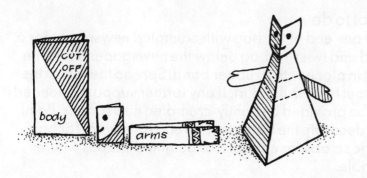

61

Cotton-pulp figures

Age range
Five to seven.

Group size
Individuals.

What you need
Cotton-pulp shapes; paints or felt-tipped pens; scraps of material or coloured foil; wool.

What to do
These pulp shapes are commercially available and are 9.5 cm high. They are ideal as figures for the corrugated cardboard crib described on page 81, and can be decorated with paints or felt-tipped pens. To make the figures more identifiable, add wool for hair and make costumes from scraps of material or coloured foil.

Paper-bag figures

Age range
Five to seven.

Group size
Individuals.

What you need
Plain paper bags; newspaper; rubber bands; paints; wool; scraps of fabric; gummed paper shapes.

What to do
Stuff one end of the bag with crumpled newspaper for a head and twist the bag below the newspaper. Hold the twist in place with a rubber band. Spread the rest of the bag out to form the skirt. If any further support is needed it can be provided by lightly-crumpled newspaper. Paint and decorate the bag as required, using wool for hair, fabric scraps for clothes and gummed shapes where suitable.

What you need
Thin card; adhesive; paints or felt-tipped pens; scraps of fabric; wool; scissors.

What to do
To make uniform figures, first cut a template, as illustrated, from a piece of scrap card, then draw round this on white or coloured thin card. The measurements suggested will give a figure 15 cm high. To vary the size, use the proportions of 3:1, body to head. Cut off the shaded parts, then curl the card as described in 'Techniques', page 87. If the body is to be painted, it is

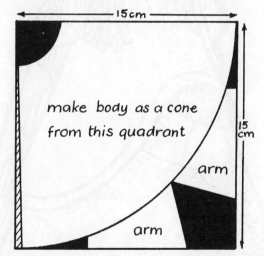

A template is provided on page 125

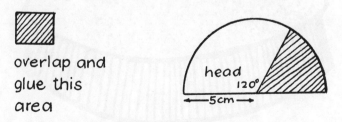

overlap and glue this area

Cone figures

Age range
Five to seven (with help).
Seven to nine.

Group size
Individuals.

easier to do this now, before the cone is raised. Overlap and glue the area indicated, then stick the head, point down, into the neck of the body.

Add the headgear (a piece of an egg carton, a patch of fur, or a crown made from a cake band, are alternatives to wool hair) and then the face. Stick the arms in place and add paper ovals for hands. Use another quadrant of a circle with a smaller diameter to make a cloak or a collar. Heads may also be made from table-tennis balls, cotton-pulp shapes or balls of crumpled paper covered with coloured paper – gather in any surplus paper with a thread wound round and glue the surplus into the neck of the body to fasten the head firmly in place.

Tubular figures

Age range
Five to seven.

Group size
Individuals.

What you need
Cardboard tubes (make your own from thin card, or use the centres of paper rolls) or empty tubular containers; paints or felt-tipped pens; Plasticine.

What to do
If you make your own tubes for these figures they can be any size: a good proportion is 2.5 times as high as the diameter of the tube. Curl the card as described in the chapter on techniques, page 87. To make the figures stand firmly, stick the lower rim to a circle of card or wedge them into lumps of Plasticine.

You may prefer to use discarded tubes (eg household containers) and cover them with paper. More variety in size may be obtained in this way. They have the advantage that they can be weighted with pebbles or sand before being dressed. Fasten the lids in place with Sellotape. It is not necessary to provide a separate head as a

face-coloured strip can be stuck at the top of the tube, or a U-shaped piece of paper or felt. Arms are also dispensable, but may be suggested by rolls of paper, with or without a pipe-cleaner core.

Pine-cone figures

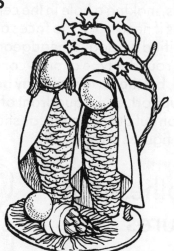

Age range
Seven to nine.

Group size
Individuals.

What you need
Pine-cones, either the common type or the thinner, oval variety – do not mix the two; cotton-pulp balls; thin card; adhesive; scraps of fabric; wool; scissors; a craft knife.

What to do
If you are using oval pine-cones, cut off the points of the cones and glue the blunt ends on to circles of card to make

them stand up. Stick cotton-pulp balls on the other ends for heads, making a hole in the centre of the ball with scissor points if necessary. No faces are needed – figures are identified by cloaks, headgear, etc.

The rounder type of pine-cone also requires a ball for its head, but the lower half may be set into a short card cone for support. Use a quadrant of a circle for this with a section cut out at the top, as shown in the instructions for cone figures on page 63.

Clothes-peg figures

Age range
Seven to nine (with help).
Nine to twelve.

Group size
Individuals.

What you need
Dolly type clothes-pegs; Plasticine; felt-tipped pens; pipe-cleaners; fabric; wool; scraps of thin card or foil.

66

What to do
Mark in the face with felt-tipped pens and dress the body by folding a strip of material round the peg and overlapping it at the back. Gather it and tie in at the neck and waist with thread. Roll a strip of fabric around the pipe-cleaner to make the arms and sleeves. Stick or stitch the pipe-cleaner to the centre of the body at the back or wind it tightly once about the neck. Hands may be suggested by sticking scraps of cotton wool or paper over the ends of the arms and painting them. Wings may be made from thin card or foil. Push the tips of the peg into a lump of Plasticine to stand the figure up.

Tubular figures with legs

Age range
Nine to twelve.

Group size
Individuals.

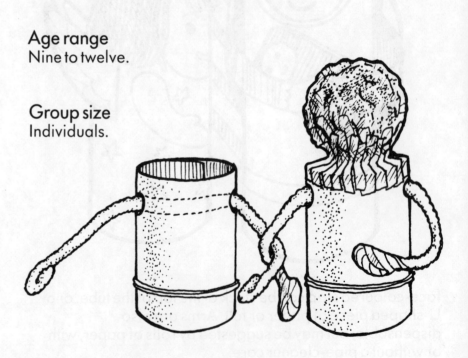

What you need

Two sturdy sticks about the thickness of a pencil; a pipe-cleaner or a 20-cm length of thin wire; a piece of thin card, 7.5 × 30 cm; newspaper; Plasticine; cold-water paste; a rubber band or Sellotape.

What to do

Because these models have separate legs, they can be made to sit. These measurements will give a figure about 20 cm tall, but the size can be varied. Roll the card into a cylinder 2.5 cm in diameter, and secure it with a rubber band or Sellotape. Pierce two small holes in the top of the cylinder and thread the pipe-cleaner or wire through them. To make the head, crumple newspaper into a small ball and cover it with another sheet of newspaper, twisting it at one end to form the neck – push this into the top of the cylinder and secure it with small strips of paper dipped in paste. Use further strips of pasted paper to smooth over the head and build up the shoulders. Leave this to dry. Stuff a little crumpled newspaper into the bottom of the cylinder, then push in the stick legs and secure them in the required position, as for the head. If the figure is to stand, press the ends of the legs into two lumps of Plasticine shaped like feet.

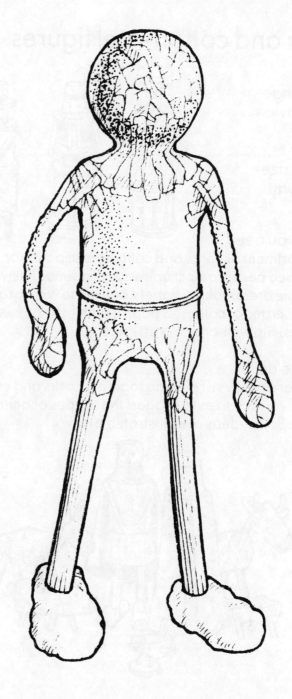

Cork and cotton-reel figures

Age range
Nine to twelve.

Group size
Individuals.

What you need
An assortment of corks and cotton reels; paints or felt-tipped pens; contact adhesive; paper adhesive; pins – both the dressmaking variety and those with large glass heads; scraps of coloured paper; matchsticks; beads; feathers; pipe-cleaners; craft knife.

What to do
Try different ways of placing together corks and cotton reels of various sizes to suggest the shapes of animals and figures. Some ideas are illustrated below.

Corks may be cut and trimmed, but it is better to use them in their natural shapes if possible. Glue or pin on small scraps of paper to suggest clothes. Pieces of pipe-cleaner make shepherds' crooks and cows' horns, and matchsticks can be used for arms. Feathers and beads can also be used where appropriate.

Bottle figures

Age range
Nine to twelve.

Group size
Individuals.

What you need
An assortment of discarded containers and plastic bottles (do not use spray bottles); adhesive; card; paints; pipe-cleaners; cotton wool; scraps of fabric, braid, wool, etc.

head cylinder in place. Add a cloak and other details, noting that for these larger figures fabric cut on the cross will drape the best.

What to do

Choose the sizes of your containers to suit the characters, for example, a squat plastic container can be adapted for a kneeling figure. A plastic bottle which has one sloping edge can suggest a character seen in profile with a long cloak or train. A tall symmetrical bottle becomes a figure seen face-on, while a more unusual shape may be suited to an angel figure.

Make the head from a cylinder of thin card made to fit the top of the bottle, roughly one-sixth of the total height. This disguises the shape of the bottle at the top and is easy to paint and decorate. Do not stick it in place until you have dressed the figure. Measure round the widest part of the bottle and add half as much again to give the width of the robe, which should be cut according to the length of the bottle, with about 2.5 cm added for turnings. Sew or stick the short raw edges together, then turn over the fabric and gather the top edge. Place the robe on the bottle, draw it up to fit, then tie off the thread. Twist together the ends of two pipe-cleaners for the arms and wind strips of paper or cotton wool round the ends for hands, then paint them. Make another tube of fabric for the sleeves, slip this over the arms and stick or stitch it centrally to the back. Stick the

Paste-sculptured figures

Age range
Nine to twelve.

Group size
Individuals.

What you need
Large, empty cereal boxes; adhesive; thin, galvanized
wire; newspaper; cold-water paste (thick cream
consistency); absorbent fabric; gold and silver spray
paint, enamel paint or emulsion paint.

What to do
Roll the cereal box into a tall cone shape, stick it in place
and trim the lower edge so that it stands steadily. Cut a
piece of wire about 60 cm long, insert it through the top of
the cone and bend it in half to form the neck. Fold back two
loops of wire for hands. Crumple a ball of newspaper for
the head, make a hole in it with scissor points and press it
on to the neck, securing it with a few strips of pasted
newspaper. Stand the model on some scrap paper and
begin to dress it. Cut or tear some strips of cloth about
2.5 cm wide and dip them in the paste one by one. Squeeze
out the surplus paste and smooth out the fabric, then wind
the strips round the arms, hands and upper body of the

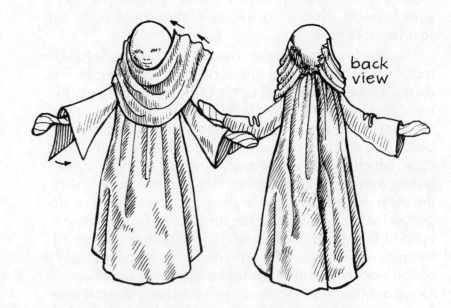

back view

70

figure. Cut a piece of fabric about 75 × 35 cm and make a small hole towards each end on one long side about 4 cm down and 23 cm from the short edges. Dip the fabric in paste, squeeze it and smooth it out as before, then drape it round the figure, pushing the arms through the holes and arranging the surplus fabric in folds. Bind the

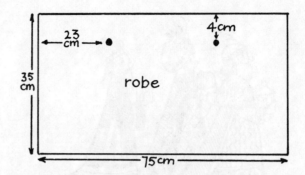

folds at the neck with thread or a narrow strip of soaked cloth. Cut an 18-cm square of fabric for each sleeve. Fold each in a triangle, soak them with paste, then drape them round the arms with the tip at the top. Cover the head or face with a small square and drape some head covering in place if required. Leave it to dry in a low oven, then paint or spray it to decorate.

Dressing nativity figures

This section will give you some ideas for dressing the characters in your nativity play. It is important to keep the materials used to scale with the figures, for example, the smaller the figure the finer the material should be. For the very smallest figures, the shapes themselves are enough to suggest clothes. Paper is often useful for dressing stylized figures. For larger, more realistic models, the following suggestions are offered.

The three kings
Robe: satin; velvet; any fabric with a sheen. The inside of old rayon ties with a pattern to scale is suitable, and has the advantage of being cut on the cross so that it drapes well.
Cloak: use similar materials; give the cloak a train.

71

Crown: each ethnic type can be given a different crown. A turban is easily made from a triangle of fabric with stuffing enclosed so that the folds can be well draped. Bring the point of the triangle towards the front. A sense of opulence can be suggested if the turban is wider than the face below it. Top the turban with a shallow gold crown and a feather aigrette.

Hair and beards: certain types of lampshade fringing may be used, or try fur fabric with the pile clipped to shape, or zigzag knitting wool from side to side below the chin.

Accessories: use scraps of gold braid or discarded bits of costume jewellery for collars and necklaces. Add ear-rings made from beads or curtain rings. Make the gifts look important. Small containers can be wrapped in foil and have sequins stuck to them. Each can be made into a different shape.

Colours: use rich, sumptuous colours such as yellow, red, emerald, blue, magenta and purple.

Shepherds
Robe: wool; coarse material to suggest sacking; pyjama-type striped material, with the stripes running downwards.

Headsquare: fine cotton, bound round the forehead with thick wool.

Girdle: cord; string; wool.

Beard: crimped wool; sheep's wool.

Crook: a twig with bent pipe-cleaners tied on to it, which are then painted brown. Do not make this too small – it should be as high or higher than the figure.

Colours: brown; dull green; dull red; neutral colours.

Joseph

Dress Joseph as a shepherd, but give him a halo, which can be made from a circle of gold card.

Mary

Mid-blue is the traditional colour for Mary's robe. She also wears a head covering, thrown back a little. This can be a lighter shade of blue. Give her long hair, parted in the middle, made from silky yarn. She also has a halo.

Baby

The baby can be wrapped in swaddling clothes and only needs a round face and a halo showing. The face may be made from a paper bead with a small stick wedged into it, which is then covered by wrapping a fleecy material around it to suggest a shawl. Bring the fabric up round the head and face, which may have one or two strands of wool for hair.

NATIVITY
ANIMALS

Folded-card animals

Age range
Five to seven.

Group size
Individuals.

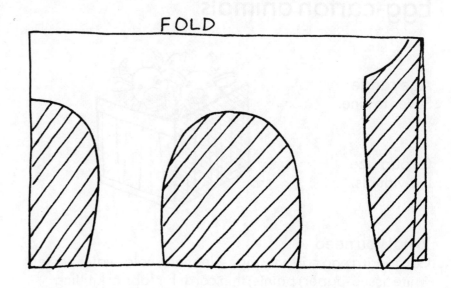

FOLD

Sheep, oxen and a donkey are the traditional animals present at the Christmas crib.

What you need
Thin card or stout cartridge paper; paints; crayons or felt-tipped pens; fur fabric, sheep's wool or knitting wool; adhesive.

What to do
For a very simple, standing two-dimensional animal, fold the card or cartridge paper in two and, on one side of the paper, draw the silhouette of the trunk, legs and tail. Place the top of the back on the fold. Draw the head and neck and cut them from a single thickness. Colour and mark in the features, then stick the head on to the body. For a little more textural interest, cover the back with fur, sheep's wool or knitting wool, which you can crimp by plaiting or twisting it tightly, wetting it thoroughly and then leaving it to dry before undoing it.

Egg-carton animals

Age range
Seven to nine.

Group size
Individuals.

What you need
Cardboard egg cartons; pipe-cleaners; cold-water paste; white tissue-paper; paints; thin card; fur fabric; knitting wool or sheep's wool.

What to do
These animals have heads and bodies only. They can be used in positions where their legs are hidden – by the stalls, by being carried by the shepherds or simply by sitting down. Cut off one section of an egg carton. Cut a square or circle of tissue-paper measuring about 12 cm in diameter and paste it. Place it over the egg carton section and press the surplus inside the cup. Repeat this once or twice, then leave it to dry. Paint it beige or brown. Cut eyes and ears from thin card, stick them on and paint them. The ears may also be set into slits in the card. Make horns for the oxen with covered pipe-cleaners.

For the bodies or necks, pierce four equidistant holes along the edge of the egg cup and push the ends of two pipe-cleaners through them. Cover this framework with knitting wool, sheep's wool or fur fabric, sewn or stuck in place.

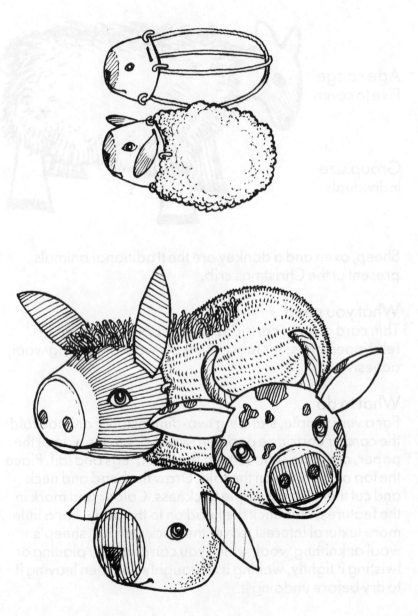

76

Woolly sheep

Age range
Seven to nine (with help).
Nine to twelve.

Group size
Individuals.

What you need
Sheep's wool; black and white pipe-cleaners; black ink or paint; scraps of black felt.

What to do
Tease out a square of wool measuring approximately 10 cm and lay it on a flat surface. Place a white pipe-cleaner across the wool and fold over the ends to hold it in place. Roll it up like a Swiss roll to form the body. Thread two black pipe-cleaners through the body and fold back the ends to create legs. Loop half a black pipe-cleaner through the folded pipe-cleaner at one end of the body and shape the face by wrapping a small amount of teased wool round it. Paint it black. Stick tiny pieces of black felt in place for the eyes. Make the ears by threading a piece of black pipe-cleaner measuring about 4 cm through the top of the head. Horns are optional; if they are required, thread a white pipe-cleaner through the head and curl the ends.

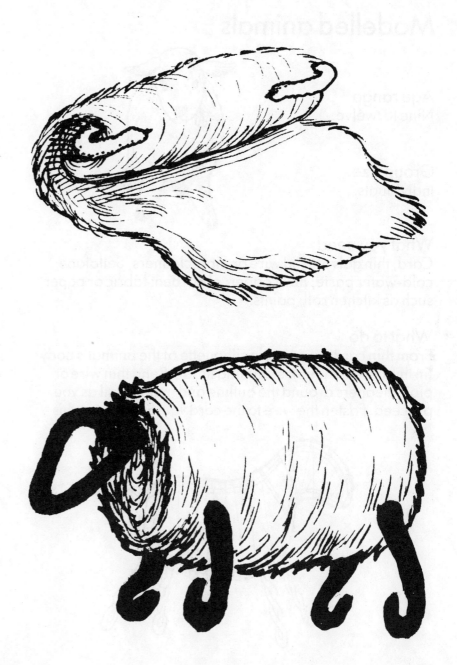

Modelled animals

Age range
Nine to twelve.

Group size
Individuals.

What you need
Card; thin galvanized wire or pipe-cleaners; Sellotape; cold-water paste; newspaper; absorbent fabric or paper, such as kitchen roll; paints.

What to do
From thin card cut a simple silhouette of the animal's body (in this case a sheep), excluding its tail. Bend thin wire or pipe-cleaners around the outline and make a tail as you proceed. Fasten the wire to the card with Sellotape – this

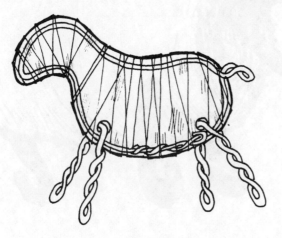

will ensure that the outline is not lost when the pasting begins. Pad out the body to make it more rounded by rolling strips of paper and sticking them in place with Sellotape. Punch two holes where the pairs of legs are to go and push a wire or a double thickness of pipe-cleaner through, bend it back and twist the surplus together.

Cut or tear narrow strips of absorbent fabric or paper or newspaper, soak them in paste and squeeze out the surplus. Then bandage them around the outline until it

becomes three-dimensional. Leave it to dry in a low oven. Add ears made out of card. Finally, paint the animal. If newspaper has been used, coat it first with white emulsion or another opaque paint, to make painting easier. Make a stand, if necessary, from lumps of Plasticine, or stick the animal to a piece of card.

CHRISTMAS CRIBS

Corrugated-card stable

Age range
Five to seven.

Group size
Individuals.
Small groups.

What you need
Corrugated card; Sellotape; moss; straw; blue tissue-paper; Plasticine; scissors.

What to do
First, work out the height of the back by measuring the height of a standing figure and adding between a third and a half of this length to it. This gives you the total height of the back from A to B. Cut the rest of the stable in the proportions suggested in the illustration. Cut a template out of scrap card if more than one crib is to be made. Place the template on the corrugated card and draw round it for several versions. If the crib is more than 30 cm high, use two thicknesses of card. Bend the sides and roof into position, and anchor them with Sellotape if necessary. Or, instead of using Sellotape, place the crib on a flat surface, weight the roof with a lump of Plasticine and fix the sides with Plasticine. You may also cut a window in the back wall and behind it stick blue tissue-paper with a silver or white star on it. Fasten clumps of moss to the roof with used matchsticks or toothpicks. Place straw on the floor.

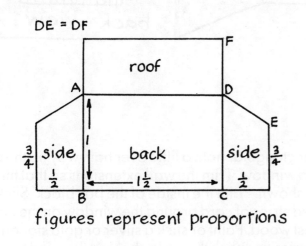

DE = DF

figures represent proportions

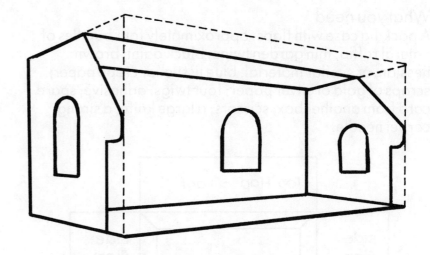

Alternatively, cover a shoe box with corrugated card. For a bigger version use a boot box or cut an existing box to shape. Cut into two corners and trim the sides as shown to give an interesting slope to the roof. Paint the inside of the box.

Packing-case crib

Age range
Seven to nine (with help).
Older children.

Group size
Whole class.

Use the packing case from a piece of domestic equipment or a grocery packing box, which many supermarkets give away – it is quicker to look round for a box of the correct size than it is to adapt one. When cutting the card, use a Stanley knife or large table-knife in a sawing motion – scissors are not strong enough.

What you need
A packing case with flaps; approximately four bundles of natural raffia; thin garden twine; black paint; brown hessian, or similar material; blue tissue- or crêpe paper; scraps of gold or silver paper; four twigs; adhesive; spare card from another box; scissors; a large knife; a strong carpet needle.

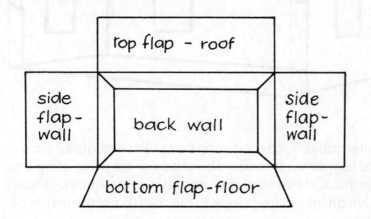

What to do
Lay the box on its side and open the flaps towards you. The top flap folds back to become the roof. The side flaps become wall extensions, and the bottom flap folds outwards for the floor extension.

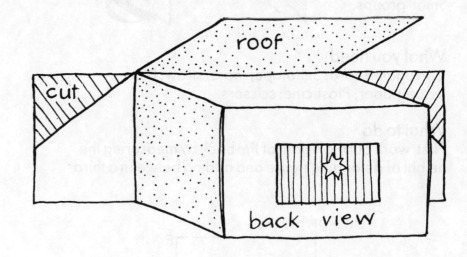

Cut a rectangular hole a little over half-way up the back wall for a window. Trim the wall extensions so that they slope as shown. Paint the inside of the box black. Stick unpainted strips of card around the window on the inside to suggest wood. Paint or stick a silver or gold star on blue tissue-paper and stick the paper behind the window.

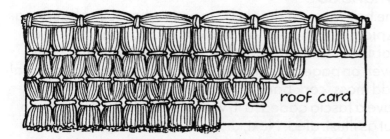

roof card

Cut hanks of raffia to fit the roof from top to bottom, allowing about 4 cm for an overhang. Sew them in place with garden twine. Alternatively, coat the roof well with contact adhesive, tie the hanks into bundles and press them in place. Sew a long hank of raffia along the apex. Anchor the roof to the back of the box with a loop of straw stuck down with Sellotape.

Use two pieces of rectangular card to make the animal stalls. Cut the card to the same height as the lower edge of the window. Fold it in half to create a V shape and stick it in place. Cut a long strip of hessian, fray the top edge and glue it from flap to flap and over the stalls. Trim four sticks and wedge them into place between the roof and the floor. Tie them to the stalls and walls with thin string, or fit them into holes made in the roof. Stick the ends to the floor with Plasticine.

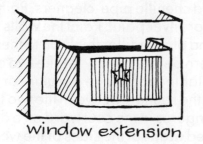

window extension

Follow-up

The floor extension can be made larger by using a semicircular section cut from another box. For a very effective window, take a piece of card and paint it black on one side. Cut a rectangular hole in it the same size as that already cut into the back wall (see page 82). Stick blue tissue-paper and a star to the unpainted side, and glue it behind the window, leaving a small space as shown.

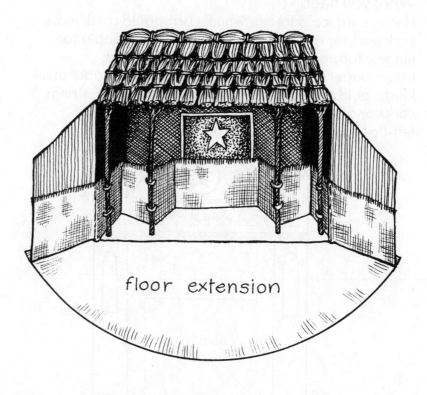

floor extension

83

Christmas crib scene

Age range
Nine to twelve.

Group size
Whole class.

This setting for a crib scene can be made to any size, but because it is constructed in card it is preferable that the tallest part is no more than 45 cm high. The taller the scene, the heavier the card needs to be. If necessary, the background may be strengthened by sticking strips of heavy card across and down the back.

What you need
Heavy card, coloured or white; corrugated card; moss, cork bark, or raffia; pins; adhesive; strong paper for hinges; fabric or paper; paints; foil; coloured tissue-paper or translucent paper; coloured paper of all kinds; gold and silver spray paint; plaster filler; string; corks and other stick-on materials to give texture; felt-tipped pens; scissors; craft knife.

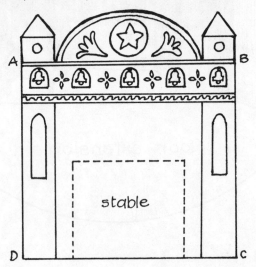

What to do
The background should be in proportion to the figures, as explained in the section on making a corrugated-card stable. First make the stable, following the instructions given on page 81, but do not cut a window in the back wall. Add moss, cork bark or raffia to the roof. The front may have a fascia added to it, with cut-out doors which open out as illustrated. Next, draw out the background to the scene. ABCD is nearly square, but can be adjusted to the size of the stable. A–B is twice as high as the stable front. To make the side wings, cut two pieces of card the height of A–D, and a little more than D–C in length. Hinge them with strong paper so that they open out to support the back. Make a courtyard paving to cover the space in between the side wings. To do this, use fabric or paper, painted or printed with potato cuts, to suggest cobble-stones.

Follow-up
Decorate the crib in the following ways. Cut out the windows, as in the illustration, and hang paper or glass balls in them. Suggest the interior of a church by making stained-glass windows from translucent paper or tissue-paper. Make bells from corks or milk-bottle tops. Make conical paper roofs for the towers, or make them crenellated, as though for a castle. Add architectural details by sticking down thick string, pasta shapes, slices of cork or curled chenille pipe-cleaners. Paint or spray them with gold or silver paint. Paint the walls to suggest bricks, or spread plaster filler thinly on to them and scrape on a brick pattern before it is dry. Make two angels and fix them on to the stable roof. Make a feature of the nativity star and fix it in the roundel between the two towers on the roof. Place the figures in the courtyard on a different level by making raised areas at the sides of the walls, using small boxes covered with material or card.

TECHNIQUES

A number of simple techniques are repeated from time to time in this book. The following are details of some of them.

Curving card

Card can be curved by simply bending it, but you risk unwanted creases. The required shape is much more easily achieved if you first stretch one of the surfaces. (Any painting or drawing which could be smudged is best done after the stretching.) Put the card on a table and hold the near side firmly with your left hand. Take a ruler in your right hand and place it edge down on the card, close to the near side, then press it firmly down while dragging the card towards you. The harder you press on the ruler the greater is the curve. If the card is not very strong you may run the risk of tearing it. To avoid this, press down lightly, but pull the card under the ruler more than once, so achieving the required curve gradually.

Curving paper

The ruler method described above may be used for large pieces of paper, but take care not to exert too much pressure on the paper in case it tears. Narrow strips, such as those used to represent hair, decorative bows or the feathers in a bird's tail, can be more conveniently curled over a table knife or scissor blade. Hold the blade in your right hand, edge uppermost, and one end of the paper in your left hand between forefinger and thumb. Position the blade edge under the paper close to your left forefinger and place your right thumb on top of the paper so that you press it against the blade edge. Pull the strip to your left, dragging it between the blade edge and your right thumb. As with the ruler method, the stronger the pressure the greater the curl. To avoid the risk of tearing, you may gently run the strip over the blade more than once. This method is particularly effective when used with gift ribbon. After curling, the ribbon can be divided to give even more ringlets simply by pulling its strands apart from one end.

Scoring card

You will need to use a sharp craft knife to score card. With your left hand, hold a flat ruler very firmly on the card. Place the ruler's edge exactly on the scoring line and run a craft knife along the line. At the same time, press the blade firmly against the ruler, which must not slip. Great care is needed. You should aim to make a cut which goes not more than half-way through the card, otherwise the joint is weakened. To achieve the required angle, bend the card away from the cut. Thin card should be cut in the way described below for paper.

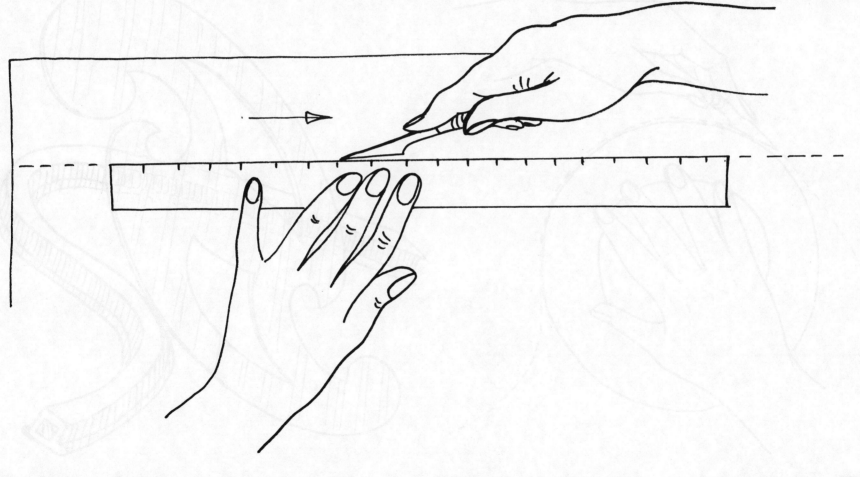

Scoring paper

It is worth taking the trouble to score paper as the result is a sharp neat crease. Scoring is the only way to achieve a circular crease. For a straight crease use a ruler, as for card. For a curved crease, a hard edge of the necessary shape needs to be used, such as a plate, or a transparent French curve or flexible ruler, both of which are available from shops that stock drawing materials. Run a pointed blunt instrument, such as a knitting needle, along the line to be scored, working as described above for card, and bend the paper away from the score. This point should be borne in mind when planning your work. Scoring is not likely to disturb any art work other than that which is most easily smudged, so it can be done after decorating.

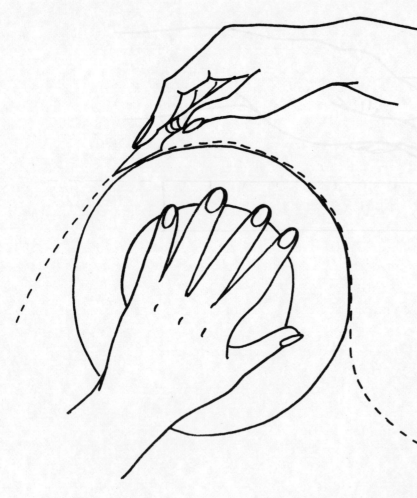

90

Crimping wool

You can make ordinary knitting wool into a curly textured mass representing hair, moss or grass, depending on the colour you choose. Crimped wool is more easily handled than straight lengths. Plait, knit or crochet the wool, using several strands together for speed. Do not bother to cast off if you knit the wool, but simply slide the stitches from the needle, which can be a large size. Dampen the work well and press it with a hot iron, or flatten it and leave it to dry on a warm radiator. Unravel the wool and it will retain its crimp.

Drawing a large circle without a pair of compasses or a template

To do this you need two people. The circle produced will not be geometrically accurate, but will be precise enough for most purposes. Take a pencil or Biro and tie a piece of string in a slack loop around it. At the other end of the string, tie another slack loop around a knitting needle, pencil or short stick. Adjust the length so that the total length of the string, including the loops, equals the desired radius of the circle. Spread the material to be marked on the floor. Place the pencil in one loop and the knitting needle or stick in the other. One person holds the looped stick or knitting needle firmly upright in the centre of the circle, while the second takes hold of the pencil and stretches out the string as much as possible. Place the point of the upright pencil on the material and mark a circle while steadily rotating the string, which must be kept taut. The slack loops ensure that the length of the string remains constant as the marking proceeds.

length of string + loops = radius

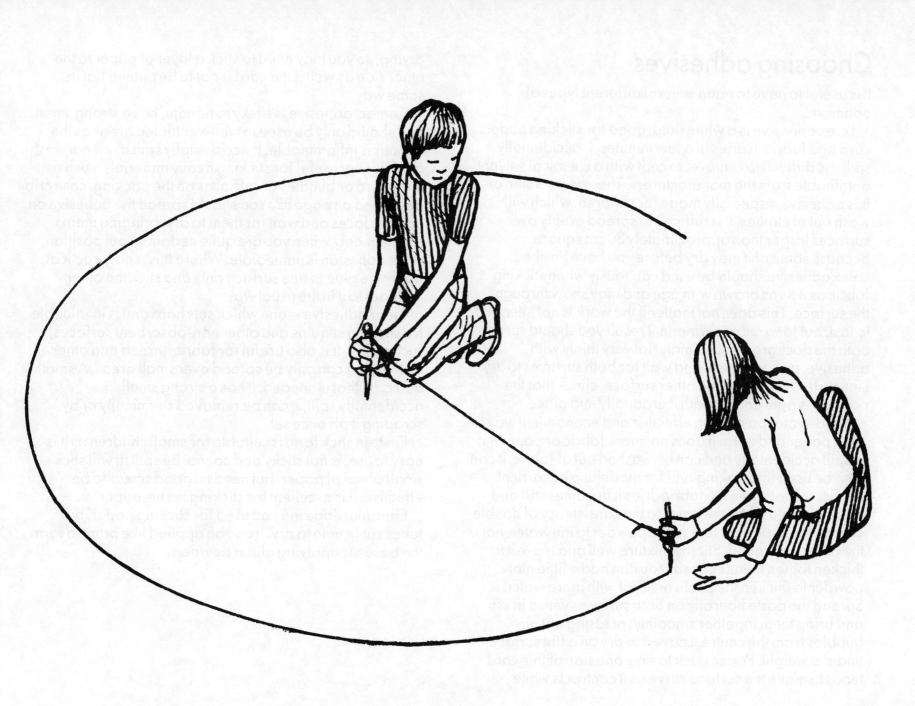

Choosing adhesives

It is useful to have to hand several different types of adhesive.

Latex adhesive is a white fluid, good for sticking paper, card and fabric. It dries in a few minutes. If accidentally spilt it is difficult to remove, except with a chemical solvent obtainable from the manufacturers. There is a version of this adhesive, especially made for children, which will wash out of clothes. It is difficult to spread evenly over surfaces larger than approximately 30 cm square, because some of it may dry before you have finished. Latex adhesive should be used cautiously when sticking fabric as it turns brown with age and may show through the surface. This does not matter if the work is not intended to last, but for a more permanent result you should spread both the background and material very thinly with adhesive, using a brush, and wait for both surfaces to dry. Line up the fabric and the other surface, check that the position is right and smooth it gradually into place.

Cold-water paste is an effective and economical way to stick paper and card. It does not mark fabric or paper if it is spilt accidentally and can be washed out of fabric. It can also be used for soaking and for modelling absorbent fabric, so that when the fabric dries it becomes stiff and retains its folds. Mix the paste to the consistency of double cream. It is important to add the powder to the water, not the other way round. Stir the mixture well and leave it to thicken for ten minutes or so. You can add a little more powder to thicken the paste or thin it with more water. Spread the paste liberally on both surfaces with a brush and bring them together smoothly, pressing out air bubbles from the centre. Leave it to dry on a flat surface under a weight. Paper stuck to only one side of thin card tends to make the surface curve as it contracts while drying, so you may need to stick a layer of paper to the other side as well if the card is not to be pinned flat in some way.

Contact adhesive is sticky to handle, has a strong smell and should only be used in well-ventilated areas as the vapour is inflammable. If accidentally spilt it will not wash out. It is very useful for sticking heavy materials, such as thick card or bundles of raffia, as on the packing-case crib described on page 82. You should spread the adhesive on both surfaces and wait for them to dry, bringing them together only when you are quite certain about position, since adhesion is immediate. Where this is not practical, apply the glue to one surface only and stick the other material to it in the usual way.

Clear adhesive is one which sets hard and is invaluable for sticking sequins and other non-absorbent surfaces, such as foil. It is also useful for fabric, thread and other textiles, but can only be spread over small areas. A small dab is all that is needed. It has a strong smell; if accidentally spilt, it can be removed chemically or by scraping it off once set.

Paste in stick form is suitable for small children as it is easy to use, is not sticky and cannot be spilt. It will stick small areas of paper, but needs a good smear to be effective. It is excellent for sticking tissue-paper.

Gum mucilage may be used for sticking paper, but takes some time to dry. It can be applied like paint to form the base for applying glitter powder.

Cutting templates

Throughout the book it is suggested that templates should be cut, for example when making the drum-shaped Advent calendar, on page 50, or the Christmas-card star on page 30. The advantage in cutting one or more templates from thin card or stiff paper is that no construction lines will show on the finished work, and work will progress more quickly and easily if the templates are passed round the class and used as outline guides.

Applying glitter

Loose glitter can be difficult to control. For an adhesive base you can apply thin liquid glue with a brush, or try pouring a little of the glue into a saucer and dabbing the surface to be decorated with it. This method works well on edges and is quick. Put some loose glitter on a large flat plate and brush the glued surface lightly in it. This is easy, but will use up the glitter quickly, so you may find it more economical to make a sprinkler from a round-lidded carton, such as a spice or baking-powder container, by pushing a few holes in the cardboard bottom with a fine knitting needle. Pour in the glitter and secure the lid in place with Sellotape applied crosswise. Sprinkle the glitter on to the glue over a large piece of paper so that afterwards the excess can be poured back into the container.

OUTLINES TO COPY

These templates, diagrams and motifs can be used for cards, design and display work. Grids are added to enable you to make scale enlargements or reductions. Don't forget the mathematical potential involved in getting children to work these out.

Snowman

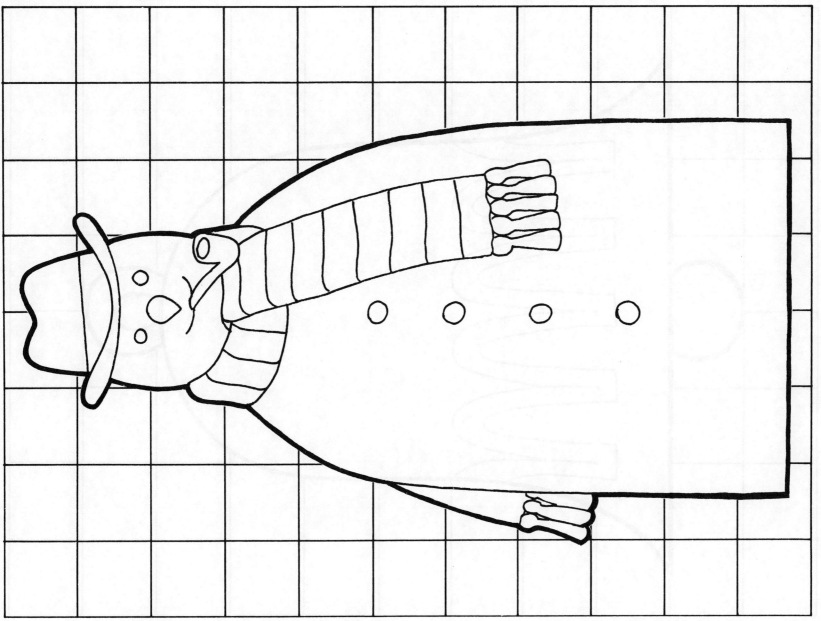

97

Bell

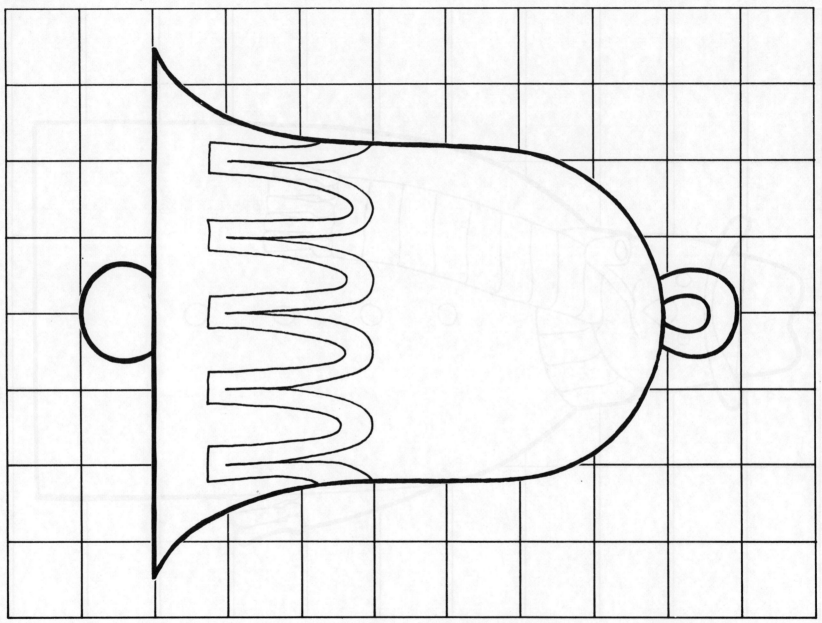

This page may be photocopied for use in the classroom and should not be declared in any return in respect of any photocopying licence.

Five-pointed star

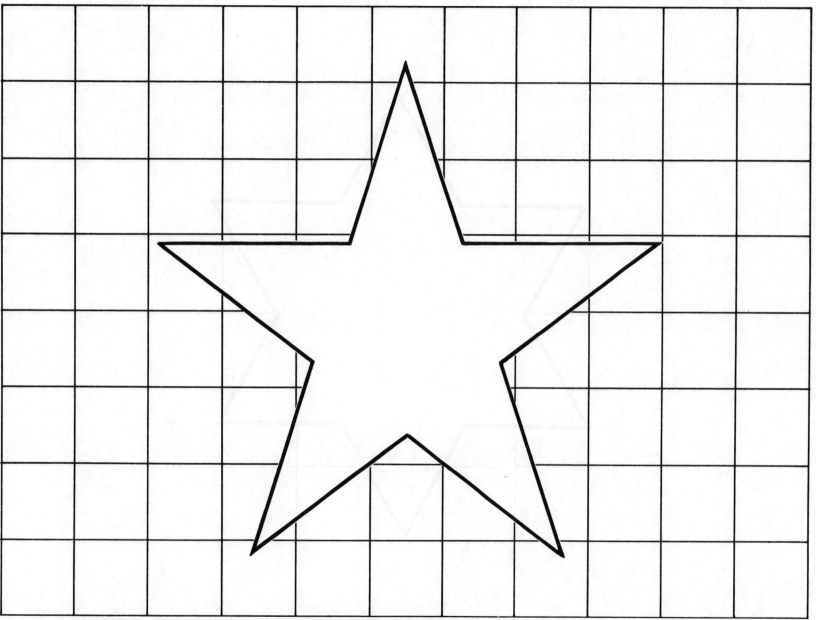

99

Six-pointed star

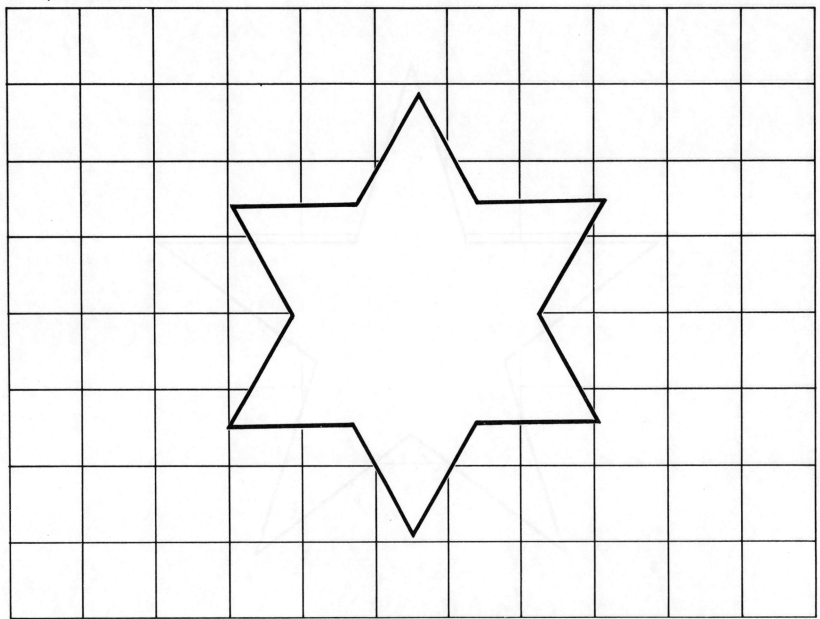

This page may be photocopied for use in the classroom and should not be declared in any return in respect of any photocopying licence.

Eight-pointed star

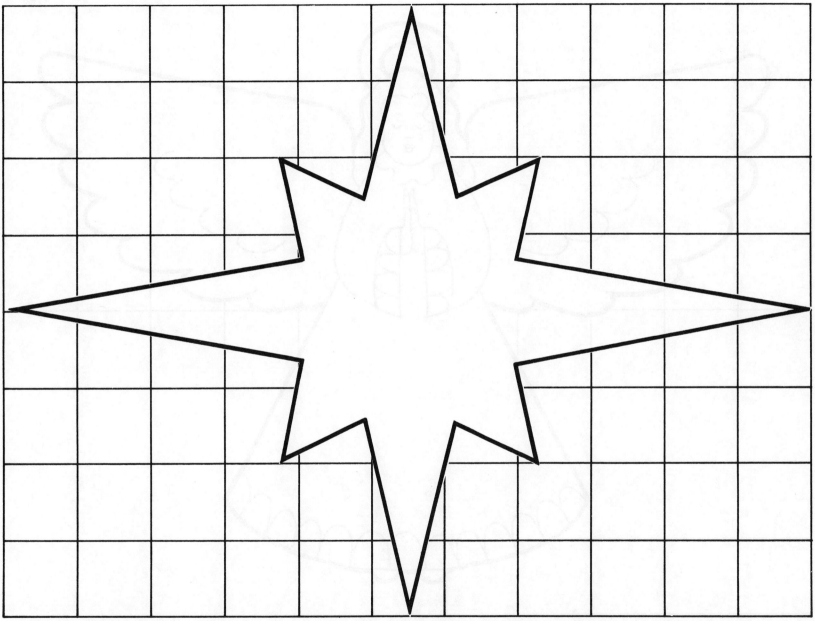

Angel

Tree

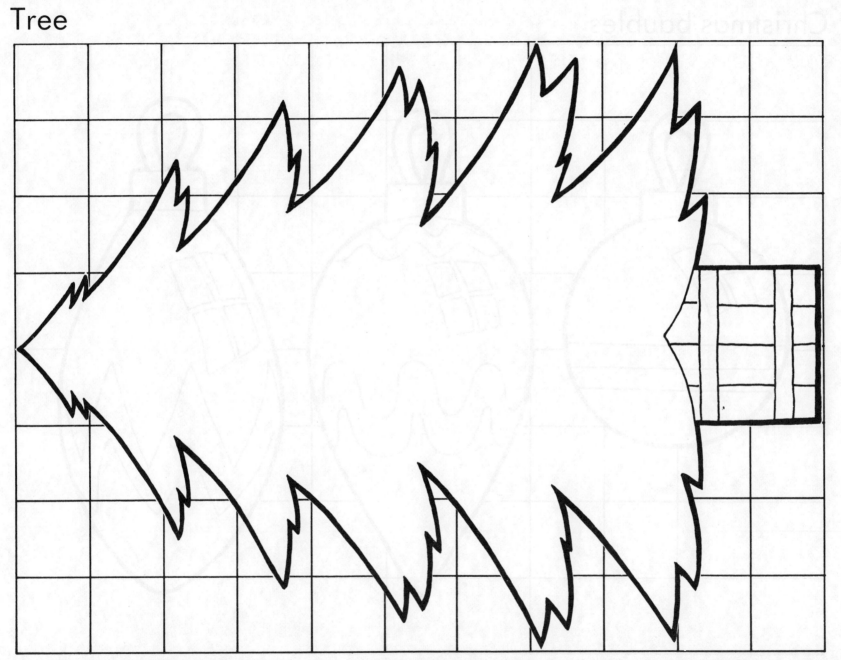

Christmas baubles

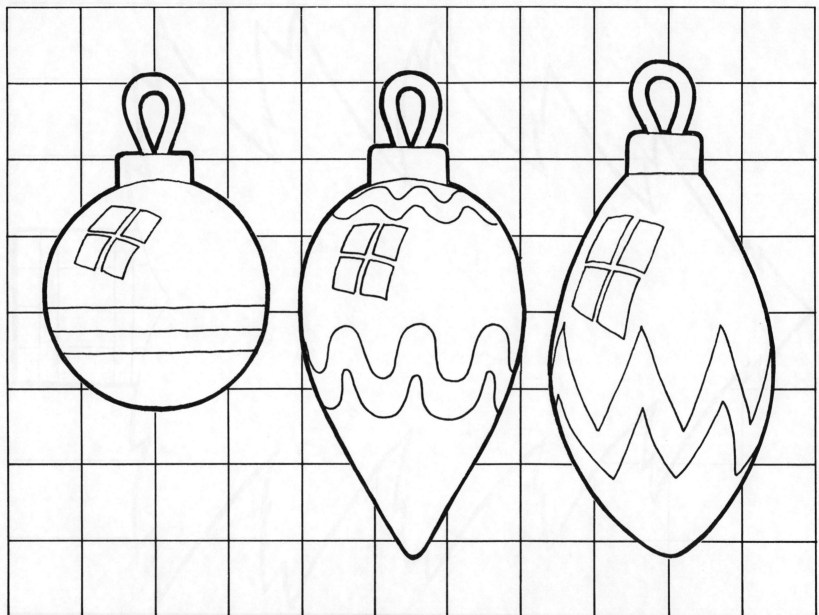

Holly

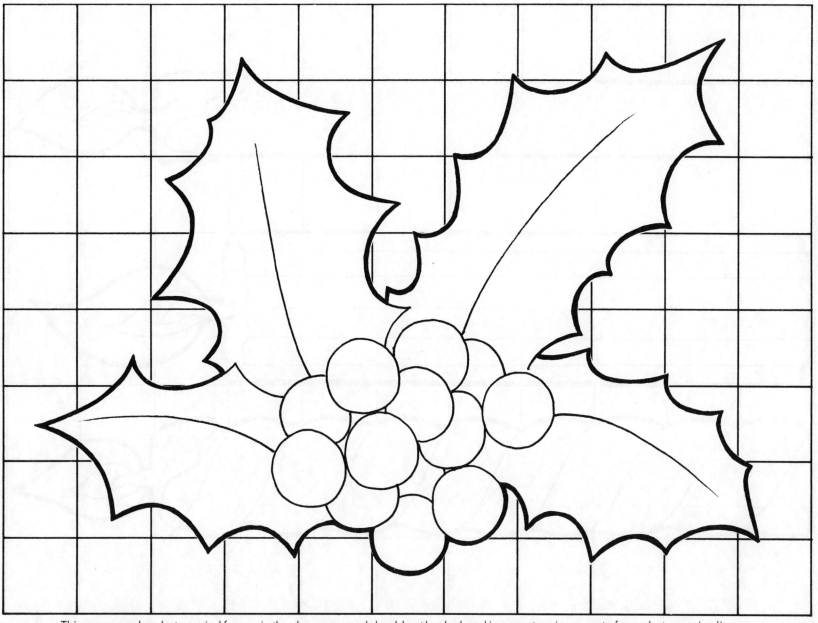

105

Candles

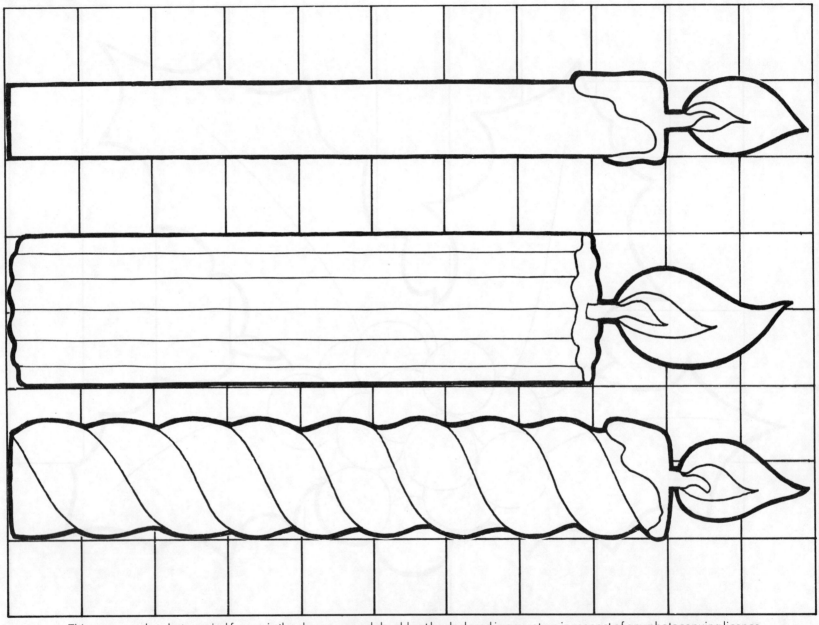

Father Christmas

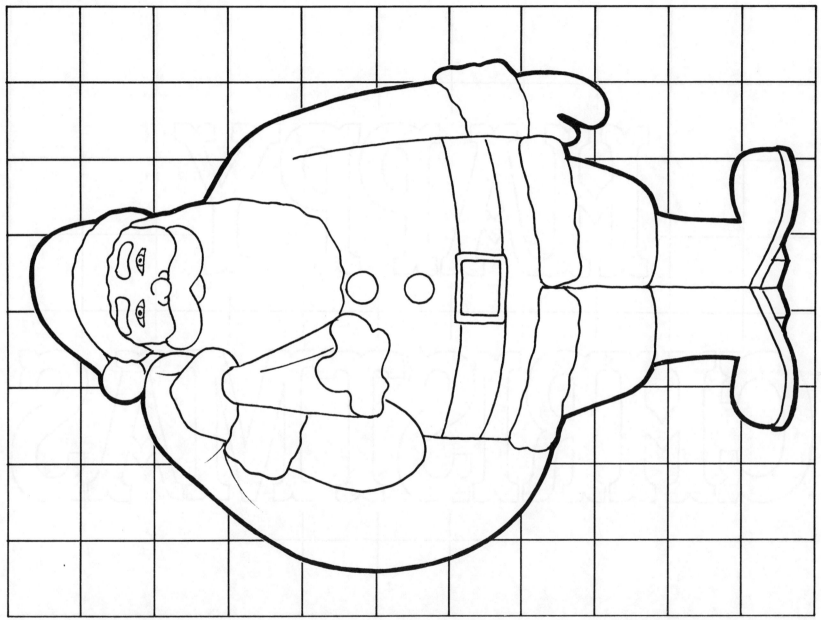

Stained-glass window

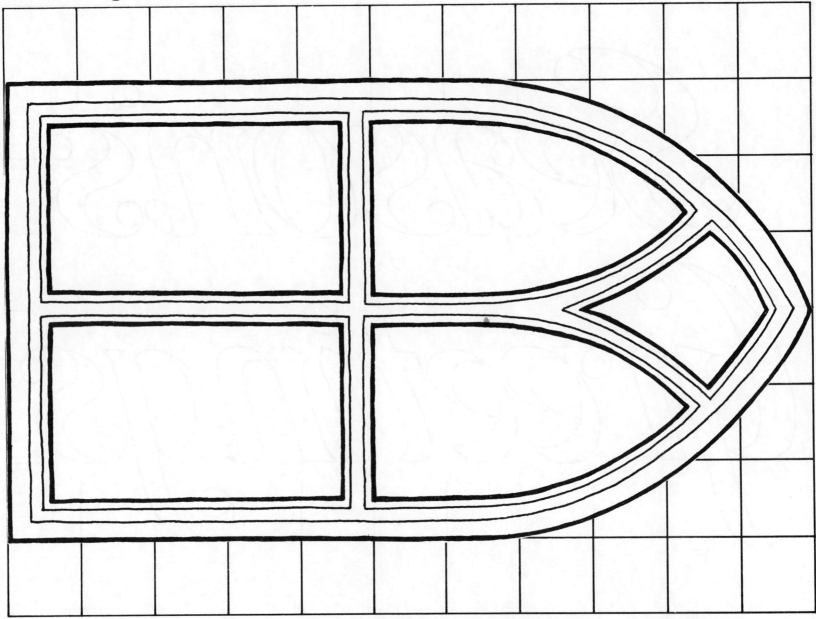

This page may be photocopied for use in the classroom and should not be declared in any return in respect of any photocopying licence.

Bethlehem

Three kings

This page may be photocopied for use in the classroom and should not be declared in any return in respect of any photocopying licence.

Shepherd

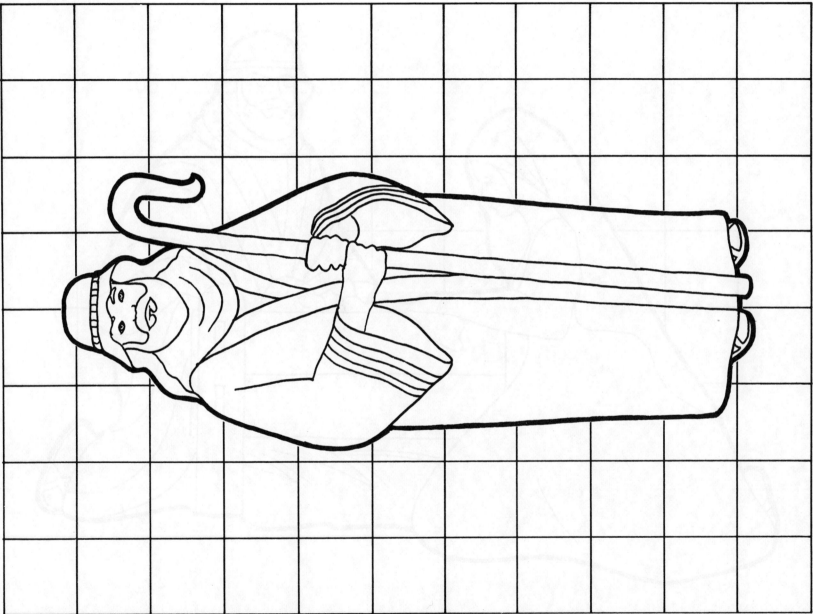

The Holy Family

This page may be photocopied for use in the classroom and should not be declared in any return in respect of any photocopying licence.

Lamb

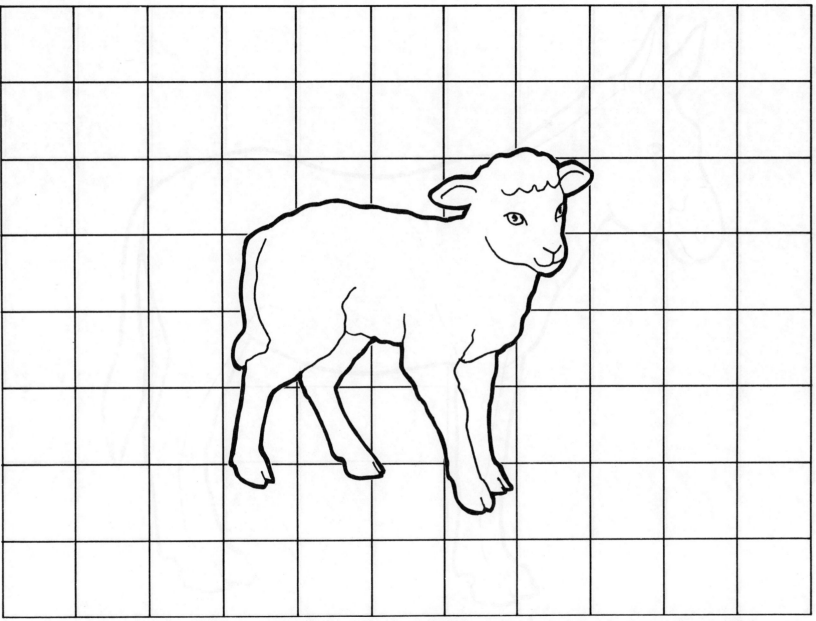

Donkey

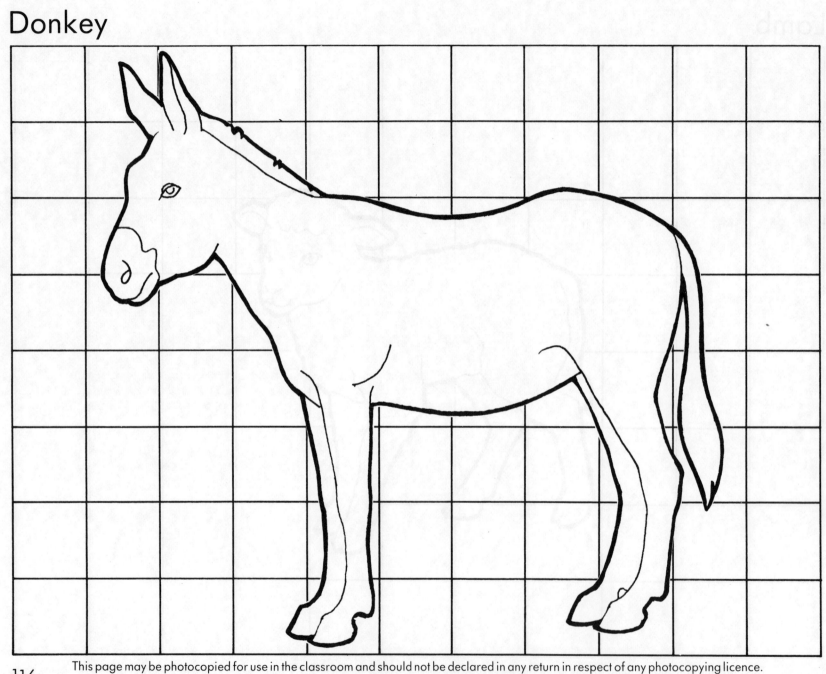

Shapes for mobiles

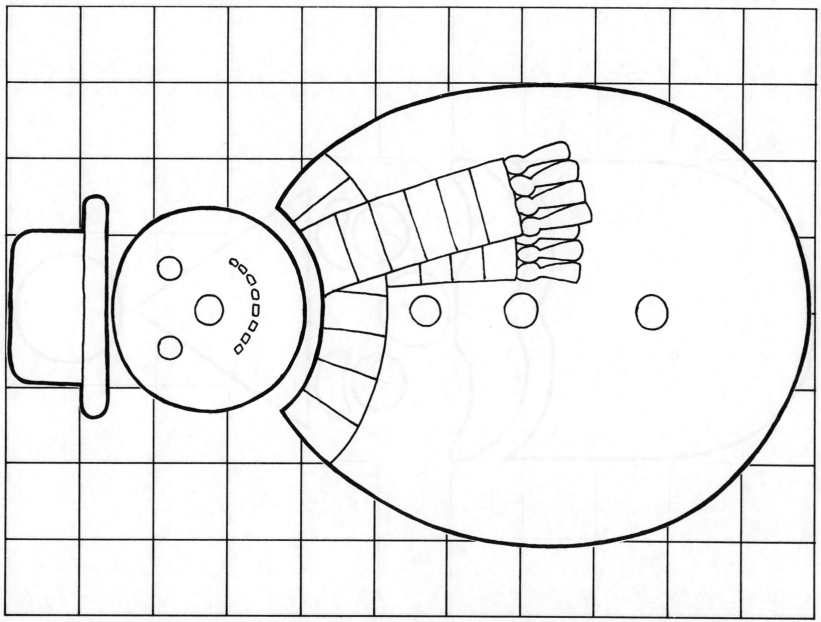

Shapes for mobiles

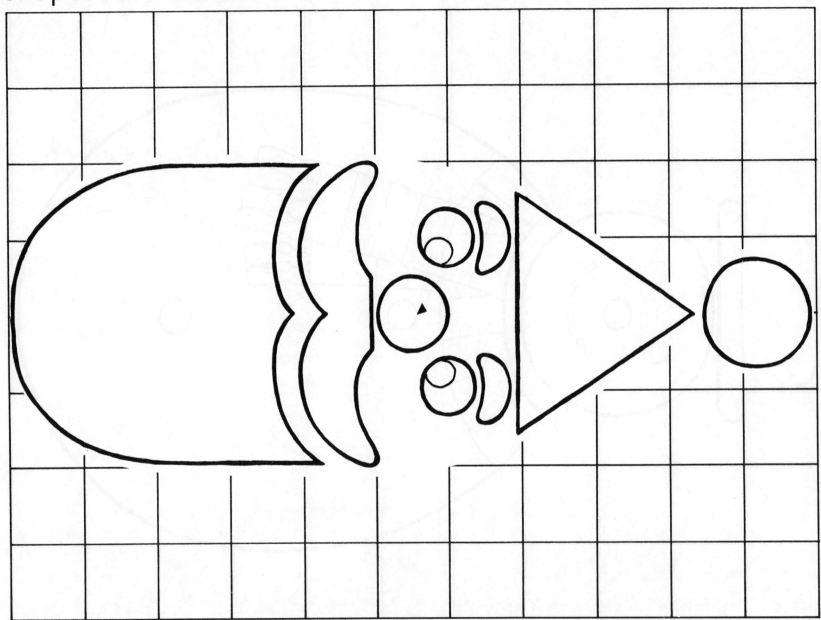

Shapes for mobiles

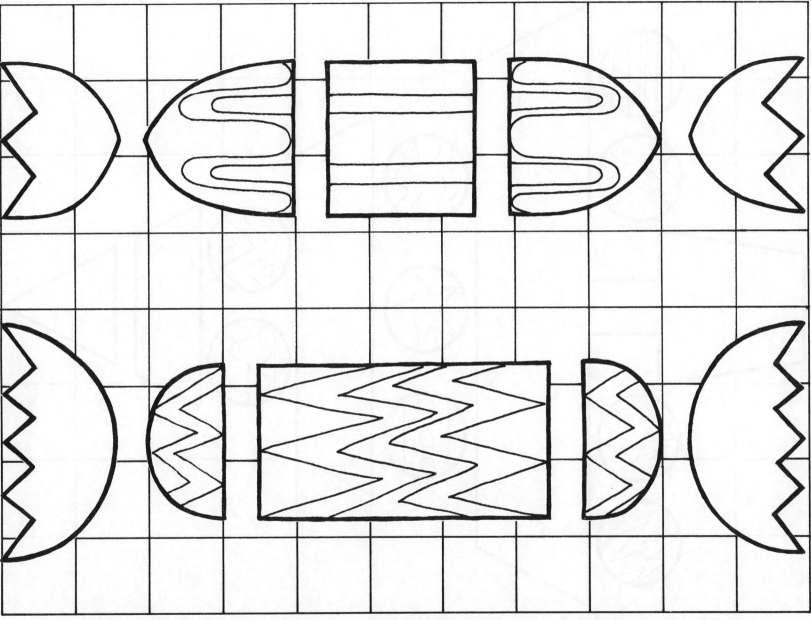

Shapes for mobiles

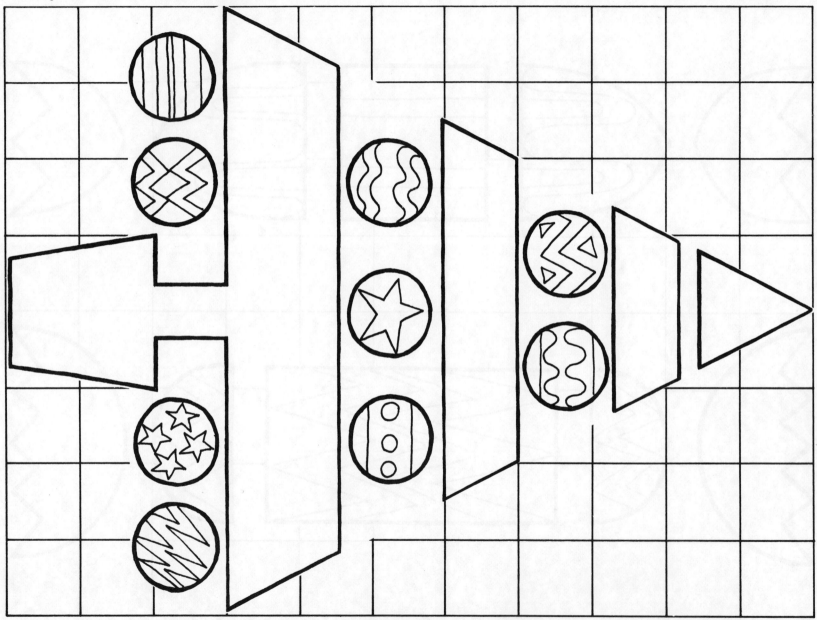

Shapes for mobiles

Snowflakes

Pyramid tree

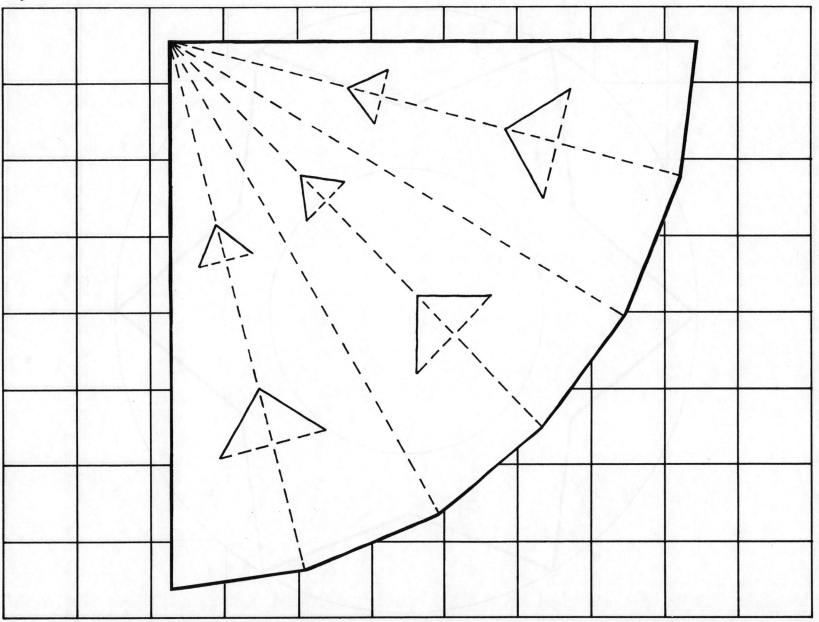

123

Christmas-card star

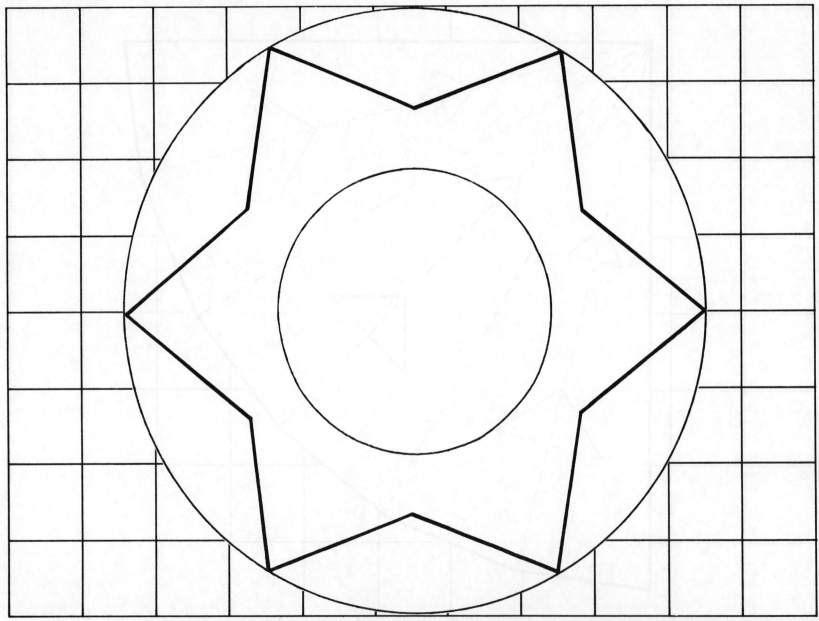

Cone figures

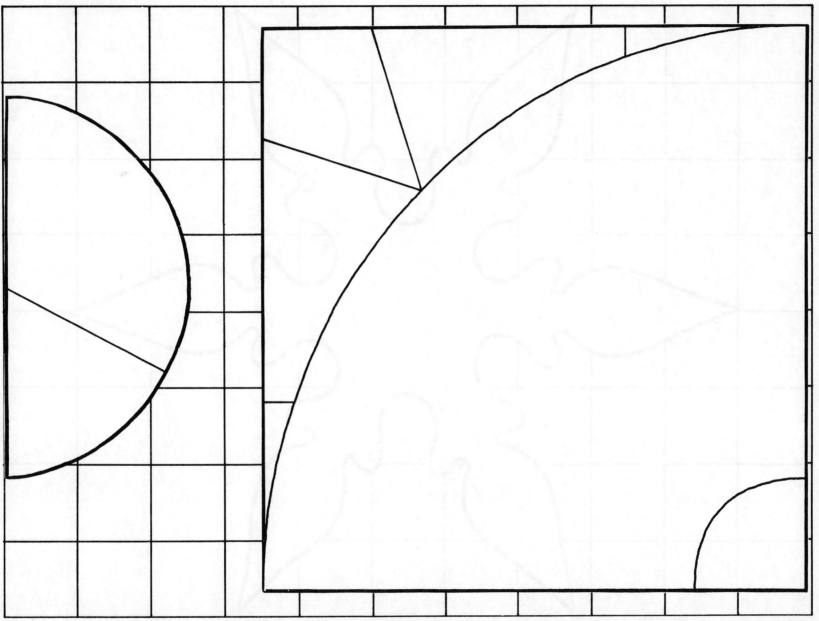

125

Tiered cone tree

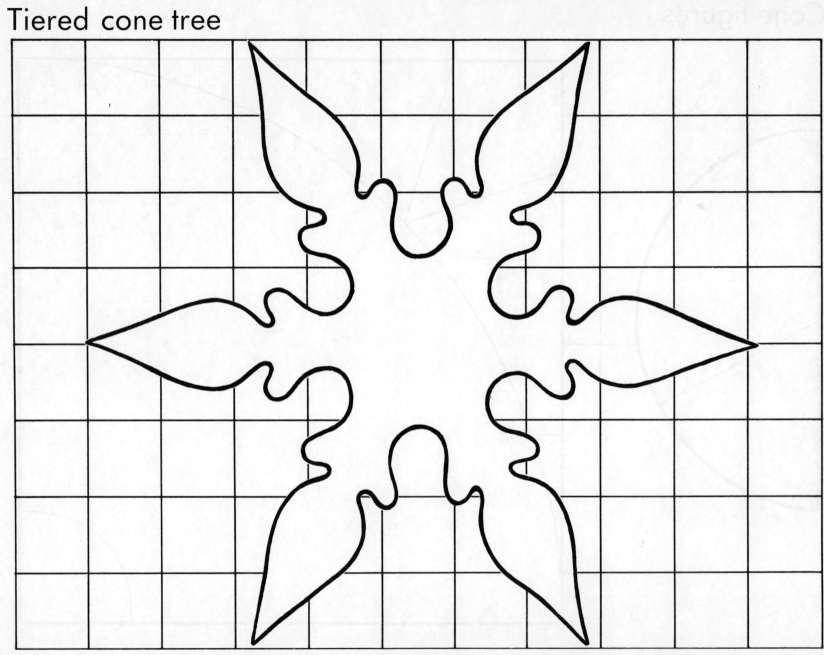

ACKNOWLEDGEMENTS

The editors and publishers extend grateful thanks for the reuse of material first published in *Art & Craft* to: David Norris for 'Three-dimensional newspaper tree'; Warren Farnworth for 'Simple cone tree', 'Egg-carton animals', 'Folded-card animals', 'Corrugated-card stable'; Ian Price and Ben Bates for 'Two-dimensional newspaper tree'; Gilly Fuest, Charlotte Gerlings and Suzy Ives for 'Drum-shaped Advent calendar' and 'Tiered cone tree'.

Every effort has been made to trace and acknowledge contributors. If any right has been omitted, the publishers offer their apologies and will rectify this in subsequent editions following notification.

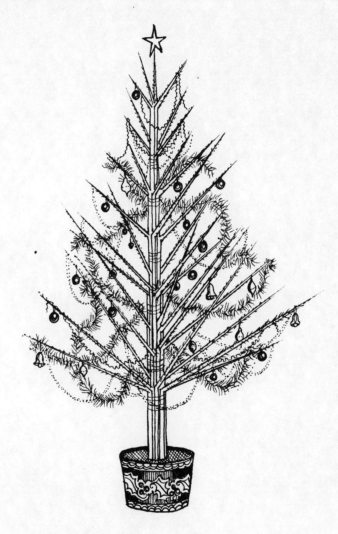